African Booty Scratcher

African Booty Scratcher

Michael Asmerom

ISBN: 1544628781
ISBN 13: 9781544628783
Library of Congress Control Number: 2017904122
CreateSpace Independent Publishing Platform
North Charleston, South Carolina

To my mother, Yeshimebet Teshome, and my two younger siblings, Semere and Fetun. It is through you guys I find the strength to keep overcoming any adversity that comes my way.

Contents

Prelude

LOOKING AT THE cover of this book, you probably did one of three things. You laughed, smiled, or were extremely confused about what you are about to read. However, if you are of African descent, you will understand the title right away. Before we delve into the title, let me tell you a little bit about myself. My name is Michael Asmerom, and I am originally from Addis Ababa, Ethiopia. I immigrated to the United States around the age of eight. As an immigrant, it felt like I hit the jackpot. America is known as some kind of paradise to foreigners outside of the United States. Growing up in Ethiopia, I heard so many wonderful stories about this country. I imagined America to be a land free of poverty, unemployment, disruption—whatever one can imagine a paradise to be. For some strange reason, when I was in Ethiopia, I thought America consisted only of white people, so when I first moved to this country, I assumed that everyone who was black was Ethiopian. When I spoke to a black man at the airport in my native Amharic language and he looked at me like I was crazy, I was baffled. I repeated myself a couple of times, thinking he didn't hear me, but after a while I came to realize he didn't understand a word I was saying; we were from different countries. It was at that moment I realized many of my assumptions about America were going to be wrong and the paradise I had in mind was not quite what I expected.

Another theory I had was that people in America lived in gorgeous mansions. Boy, I was wrong! I remembered arriving at my new home in Harlem, New York. There were heaps of littered dirt around the block and a couple of people loitering in front of the building. Well, you shouldn't judge a book by its cover (except the cover of my book, because it's really good). Anyway, I thought the inside of the building was going to be better than the outside. You guessed it! I was wrong again, although it was much better than back home. I was excited to see the bathroom. It had a toilet where I could actually sit down and do my business. It was not my first time seeing this type of toilet in an apartment. In Ethiopia, such luxury could be found in restaurants, theaters, luxury apartments, and other places, but not in my home. When we needed to go to the bathroom, there was one bathroom for the whole community of about twenty to thirty people. In Ethiopia, I lived in government-owned homes; however, at the private homes in Ethiopia, you could find a beautiful bathroom inside. It was not a toilet either, it was a hole in the ground that you had to squat over—and have excellent aim, so everything that you disposed of from your body landed in the hole. Also, you had to be very careful not to fall backward; it would not be a pretty image for you or your bum. Anyway, that problem is now far in the past, as I have a comfortable toilet that I can sit on and do all my business safely and comfortably.

Before coming to America, as I said I had many assumptions about what life in America would be like. Nevertheless, never in a million years did I imagine that I would come to America and face many challenges and feel less than a human being. Never would I have imagined coming to America and wishing I was back in Ethiopia. Whenever I had a chance to talk to people in Ethiopia about my problems in America it never really went well. It's like someone that hit the jackpot for millions of dollar complaining about having bills. It was just incomparable to them and I never got any sympathy from them. Never would I have understood the difficulties of growing up with a mom that didn't conform to the American lifestyle, and raised me as I was still in Ethiopia. So with all these challenges that was before me, did I survive or go back to Ethiopia? What was it like growing up "African" in America?

CHAPTER 1

— ❖ —

Adapting

HARLEM, NEW YORK. Usually, this is the part where people begin to describe where they lived. I would love to describe the landscape, food, infrastructure, and tourist attractions, but I can't. Growing up in an African household, I was never allowed to go outside. Or rather, my life consisted of only school and home. My mom always made sure that after school, I came straight home, which meant I couldn't explore the depths of the city. It didn't matter much anyway, because I lived right across the street from my school.

I started school in America in the second grade, whereas I had been in the third or fourth grade back in Ethiopia. It was toward the end of the year that I started attending school. I remember the teacher introducing me to the class. Well, at that time, I didn't know she was introducing me, because I didn't understand English. I'm just assuming she was introducing me. I immediately went to the back of the class and got a seat for myself. I could see all the kids looking at me, turning in their chairs, eyeing me as I walked to the back to find a seat. After I sat down, the teacher continued with the lesson. I wish I could tell you what she taught in class that day, but I have no idea. In fact, that was how most of the days in school were for me when I started. I sat there for hours, staring at the teachers, wondering what in the world they were talking about. I was so enthusiastic about learning. First I had to learn to read and write in English before I could start to understand my teachers and engage in class activities.

However, I found a challenge tougher than learning to read and write: it was adapting to the food. I remember lining up for breakfast, and on my tray were pancakes, potatoes, and cereal. I got my food and sat at the end of the table in the cafeteria by myself. I looked over to my classmates to see how they ate their food. First you open the cereal, pour the milk, and eat it with the spoon. Sounds simple, right? Not for me. Opening the milk was a struggle, as there was a specific way to open the carton. In fact, there were clear directions on the milk carton on how to go about this. After struggling for some time, I managed to fumble open the carton and pour some milk onto the cereal, and began to eat my breakfast. Instantly, I noticed all the kids looking over at me and laughing. All I could think to myself was, What foolish thing have I done now? It turns out I used chocolate milk instead of white milk. I guess there was an unspoken law that forbade this. So with that experience and a few others along the line, I concluded that in America, people acted like there was only one way to do things.

Often I would go for periods of time without eating, and when I did eat food, my stomach would hurt. Growing up in Ethiopia, I was such a picky eater, and to this day, I am still the same. It's only on the rare occasion when I will try new kinds of food. Back home, if I didn't like what was in the house, I could go to my neighbor's or another family member's house to eat. America was different; we didn't have much family, so whatever was in the house was what I had to eat, and it was the same principle when I was in school. Therefore, if I was going to survive in America, I would have to adapt to the food right away.

I recall eating pizza one day. I felt immense pain in my stomach. I went to the bathroom to take a number two, hoping that would make me feel better. I wish somebody had advised me that you don't do number two in school, because the kids will torment you. That was one of many lessons I carry with me to this day, although nowadays I don't really apply that rule much since I am attending college. After using the bathroom, I did not feel better. As I went back to class and sat down, the teacher noticed that I looked off. At that time, I still did not understand English. I could see the confusion on the teacher's face as she was looking at me; she was probably wondering how the hell she was going to communicate with me to figure out what was wrong. As she approached me, I was nervous as well, because I knew I would have to respond to her. I said a prayer in my head, hoping she would walk right past me. I guess God had more important issues to handle. She took me to the hallway and probably asked me if I was okay. I started rubbing my stomach to let her know that something was wrong there. She may have assumed that I was saying I was hungry, because she brought me a peanut butter and jelly sandwich. I shook my head to let her know that the problem was not that I was hungry. I was taken to the office, they called my mom to pick me up, and she came immediately. When I got home, I went to the bathroom, staring at myself in the mirror as I watched tears trickle down my face. I didn't enjoy a thing about America. The food was not what I thought it would be, the language was hard to learn, and I didn't have any friends. When I was in Ethiopia, I had asked many questions about America. I realized that my family members had just told me what I wanted to hear, and not the unfortunate reality. That's what I got for asking people who had never been to America in the first place. Google would have come in handy for me back then.

The next day, when my mom took me to school, the teacher told her we were going on a field trip and she had to sign a permission slip and pay five dollars. After she did as the teacher instructed her, she wished me a good day and promised that I would have fun. We got on a school bus and headed to the aquarium. Once we got to the aquarium, I was so amazed at what I was seeing. It was so cool, but I must admit I was scared that the tank would break and all the animals would escape and eat my little self. I was so amazed by all the cool animals I saw. When I was in Africa, I was oblivious to any animal that wasn't on land. Visiting the aquarium helped me expand my knowledge of animals besides dogs and goats.

After visiting all the floors in the aquarium, it was time to eat lunch. The problem was, I did not have lunch. My mother did not really understand that when students had trips, we needed to either purchase or bring food from home. As we sat on a park bench and students began to devour their food, the teacher noticed that I wasn't eating. She called me over, and walked toward a vendor who was selling food. She asked me if I would eat a hot dog. Now, at that time, I was not oblivious to English completely and I was learning some basic English phrases. For example: hi, hello, bye, cat, dog, etc. I asked the teacher, "What?" and she asked me again if I wanted a hot dog. I was in shock, because I could not believe people in America ate dogs. I shook my head for a good thirty seconds so she could fully understand that there was no way on earth I would eat a hot dog. In addition, after seeing the food, I wondered what part of the dog these people were eating. Nonetheless, I pointed to the water and gave her a thumb up to let her know water would be just fine for me.

I couldn't wait to tell my family about my day. Once I got home, I told them about all the cool animals I saw in the aquarium and how the teacher tried to make me eat a dog. All my family members gasped, and my mother asked me if it was a hot dog. I responded yes, and she started laughing hysterically. I was bewildered that my mother could laugh at such an atrocity. My mother explained to me it was not really a dog, it was just a name that was given to the food. I responded that either way, I would not eat it. I mean, who came up with this brilliant idea to name the food hot dogs? My family was laughing uncontrollably at my expense. I did not understand why my older brother and sister were laughing at me, especially since my sister had embarrassed herself not too long before in the hospital. Let me tell you what happened. My brother, my sister, and I were in a hospital room. The doctor was talking to my sister and asking her tons of questions. He asked her if my brother and I were her siblings. To my and my brother's surprise, she answered no. My brother and I looked at each other as if there was something she knew that we did not. The doctor asked her if we were not her siblings, then what were we to her? She responded that we were her brothers. My brother and I started laughing hysterically; the doctor could not help but laugh as well.

The next day of school, I was assigned an ESL teacher. ESL stands for English as a second language. I don't know why they waited so long to assign me a personal teacher. I worked tirelessly and twice as hard as my peers to catch up with them. I read countless books. I have to credit the acceleration of my learning English to the countless hours I spent watching cartoons. My favorite cartoons were "Dragon Tales," Arthur, and Barney. Now, this is where it gets a little tricky. In Ethiopia, there were tons of kids' shows that I watched on television, but none with animation. So when I came to the United States and saw shows such as "Dragon Tales," I believed they were real! I thought I would go somewhere and bump into Ord or Cassie. Don't judge me; I was very clueless, to say the least.

By the time I reached the fourth grade, I was beginning to speak pretty solid English. However, as I was learning English, I began to forget my native language, Amharic. In my mind, I did not really care too much, because I spent almost 90 percent of my time speaking English. When I talked to my mom, I often mixed English with Amharic. Not to show off or anything, but for the simple fact that I knew how to say some words in English that I did not know in Amharic. However, my mother reminded me quickly how important it was that I did not forget Amharic. It was the core of my culture, and it was something to be proud of. If I forgot Amharic and only knew English, I would be like everyone else. I would have nothing to offer more than my peers in school. Therefore, my mom instructed me that I could only speak Amharic at home and English when I was out. If I failed to follow that rule, let's just say there would be some repercussions to remind me. Looking back at it now, I am extremely grateful that she implemented that rule, because I am able to communicate with people back home more freely and I am able to state that I am bilingual on my resume.

By the time I reached fifth grade, I was nearly fluent in English. I began to shine during class, and I would always be eager to participate. I made a few friends, and I was adjusting to America better than a year or two before. That year, I began to play my first instrument: the drums. Another example of some of the stereotyping I faced. Apparently, Africans are great drummers. Although there is some truth to this, we do not come into this world playing the drums. I swear, I felt that they thought that instead of the doctor spanking the baby, he gave the child a drum. When my music teacher asked the students if they would like to play any instrument, my classmates immediately turned around and suggested that I play the drums. To their surprise, I was not as proficient as they assumed I would be, the reason being that it was my first time playing the drums.

I also attempted to make the basketball team. The key word is "attempted," because I did not play very well. In Ethiopia, and in the majority of the world, the number-one sport is soccer. I remember that back home, I would play soccer from the time the sun came up to the time the sun went down. The crazy part was, we didn't even have a real soccer ball. We made a ball out of whatever we could find. Most of the time, our ball was a bunch of plastic put together with newspaper. The lack of resources did not stop us from loving the game. We used literally anything to have a game of soccer. We found rocks or bottles to make goals. We were very creative, and we definitely knew how to have fun. I remember we would organize races on the block, and we would make medals from scratch after being inspired watching the Olympics. We took bottle caps from beer and other glass bottles and beat them with a rock until they were completely flat. Afterward, we put a hole in the top. We took the silver colored foil from a cigarette pack and covered the cap completely. Finally, we took any string we could find, and boom, we had a medal. When I came to America, I lost that sense of creativity, because you can just go to any store and buy whatever you need. When I was in Africa, I was always outside playing with my friends. But America was a bit different; because of the advancement of technology, people stayed home and played video games.

Anyway, with my involvement in fifth grade, I began to have sort of a normal life, like any American. By normal, I mean I just adapted to my surroundings. When I graduated that year, I was elected Student of the Year and I got the Triple "C" Award from New York Attorney General Eliot Spitzer and many other awards. Many students wrote in my yearbook about how proud they were of my accomplishments and how far I had come from being the scared kid in the back who didn't say a word to who I was today. Of course, there were some who were not very nice, writing things like "Good luck with middle school, teacher's pet." The most notable one I remember was someone telling me "Good luck in middle school to my favorite African booty scratcher." Well, at least he said "favorite," right?

CHAPTER 2

Bullying

"STUPID AFRICAN BOOTY scratcher." "Go back to where you came from." "Is everybody from Africa skinny?" "You are so poor." This book went from being humorous to a little serious, huh? Those top four statements are just some of the many that haunt me to this day. Do you want to know something funny? Even now, I do not have any idea what "African booty scratcher" means. I don't know how kids in the second grade understood it and had the guts to insult me. I remember the first time someone insulted me by calling me an African booty scratcher. Wait, I am lying. I didn't know English at the time, but looking back on it now, I know that's what they were saying when they pointed and laughed at me. Around the third grade, when I first started learning English, and I got called African booty scratcher in the cafeteria, I was confused, to say the least. "Booty" is slang for "butt." "Scratcher" means "one who scratches." So I was sitting there dissecting what my peers were saying to me. I remember wondering if they were saying that I scratched my butt. If they were, why didn't they just say "Michael booty scratcher"? Why did it have to be "African"? In addition, what is so funny about an African booty scratcher? What I found amusing as I got older was that a kid didn't even have to be from Africa to be called an African booty scratcher. You just had to appear to have really dark skin and fit any perception of what one might think an African looked like. For a long time, I thought that "African booty scratcher" was a special name for me, until I started having friends of African descent and they shared similar stories.

Being called an African booty scratcher was nothing compared to the many other insults I faced. I remember crying every day once I started second grade in America. I hated being in America; it was definitely nothing like I had expected. If you had told me when I was in Ethiopia the challenges I would have to face, I would have just laughed. White people were not mean; they seemed so nice on television. In the previous chapter, I spoke about how I perceived America to be filled with only white people. I couldn't imagine why someone would be mean to someone purely for the hell of it. In my culture, discipline and respect were valuable features, and my parents stressed the importance of those two traits daily while I was growing up. No matter if you were a kid or an elder, you had to show everyone the same respect and discipline. If you dared to disrespect anyone, and I mean anyone, and that person somehow had a correlation to your parents, it meant huge punishment. And by punishment, don't for a second think it was a time-out or a simple "go to your room."

I now understand that as I became more educated, I had ample culture shock. Where I went wrong was in not expecting hardship, struggle, and inequality. However, how was I supposed to have such perceptions when they had painted American to be picture-perfect in my head? Due to the bullying I have faced in most of my American life, I am very fast with my mouth. I am usually the funniest person in the room, as I am sure you've noticed from reading thus far. I realized that going to the bathroom to cry and playing the victim were not going to work. Of course, I was not able to develop this trait until I became fully proficient in the English language.

Most of the time, I was bullied for being of African descent because of the differences between me and all my peers. It was from there I took school seriously and participated in class, or read rather than played during recess. I was bullied constantly because of what I was wearing. Although I went to a uniform-wearing school from second to twelfth grade, I was still judged. So even at a uniform school, they would judge you based on the brand of your shirt and pants. Even though we were wearing the same exact thing from top to bottom, yours had a name brand and mine didn't, so I was subjected to getting bullied. Growing up in New York, I came to realize that sneakers were a big part of the culture. Most of the time, instead of looking you in the face, kids looked down to see what you were wearing.

I remember at the start of third grade, my mom bought me sneakers with a pink heart on the side of the sole. Now, my mom didn't know any better; all she knew was that I needed new sneakers and she got them for me. She didn't know about brands such as Air Jordan, Nike, Adidas, etc. Well, she did, but there was no way on earth she would spend hundreds of dollars on a pair of sneakers. All that mattered was that I had decent-looking shoes that covered my feet.

It was the first day of third grade, and I had my sneakers and my ironed uniform. I was at the cafeteria eating my cereal with *white* milk; I was not going to make the same mistake twice. I also made sure to grab some pancakes. I was excited for school that day. I was excited to continue learning English and hoping to have a better year than the previous. It was the third or fourth period, during rug time. One of the kids saw the pink heart on my sneakers, and soon enough the news spread like wildfire. It was time for lunch, and I grabbed a peanut butter and jelly sandwich and chocolate milk. I noticed all of my peers continuously staring at my feet and making remarks. I had made three mistakes. One, I was not wearing brand-name sneakers. Two, they were pink. Three, there was a heart on the side. I was so confused. What do I do now? This was just getting ridiculous.

In Ethiopia, if I were wearing what I wore the first day of third grade, I would have been glorified. Also, in America there was another unspoken rule that only girls wore pink and only boys wore blue. Anyone who broke this code would indeed get bullied. Growing up in Ethiopia, there was no such thing. You would wear what fit. Of course, there were materials made specifically for girls or boys; however, when it came to colors, it did not matter. Who had time to be worried about that when you were faced with real-life problems such as poverty, hunger, and sickness? Even if you didn't have to face such issues in Ethiopia, not many people were materialistic and worried about what you had on versus what you were thinking.

I went home that day and cried to my mom. The thing about African mothers is that they are not as sympathetic as many parents from different cultures. It wasn't that she didn't have sympathy for me, but instead, she was teaching me to develop a thick skin. What she was more flustered about was the reason I was crying. She could not believe that kids would make fun of me for those reasons. African parents, like most parents, are very protective of their kids. She went to the school the next day to talk to the teacher. However, there was only so much a teacher could do. In addition to that, when you "snitch" on your peers, it will get worse, which it did for me. "Snitches get stitches," I heard throughout that day. I am amazed how much those kids knew at that age.

What agitated me the most was the fact that those kids looked just like me. We all had the same body parts, and yet they still made me feel inhuman. I questioned my existence every day. I would come home and really wonder what life was about. Why are we here on earth? Why is there so much hatred? What was I brought here in this world to do? Would it matter if I died? I had such a lack of self-confidence, I would go to class, sit at the back, and just put my head down. I tried to block out all the negativity. It was tough sitting at the back and thinking about how they were probably looking at me, judging me for not having the same things they had. I was defensive even when people were being nice to me. For example, when somebody called me by my name: "Hey Michael, how are you?" In my mind, I thought they were saying "Hey African booty scratcher, how are you today?" I was recently at a conference and the speaker said something that resonated with me. She said, "In the absence of empathy, it is easy to dehumanize. If we dehumanize, it is easy to objectify. It is easier to talk about objects." This was very touching to me, because I realized it was hard for people to show sympathy or understand a culture they had no knowledge of.

My peers often asked me how I had such a "normal" name. I knew they meant to ask how I had a name that many Americans had and that was easy to pronounce. I often reminded them that where I came from, their names would not be considered "normal" either. My last name, Asmerom, was not "American." The kids often made fun of me by shouting "ass-moron." Literally, they took anything I had and turned it negative to try to break me down.

Americans tend to have a particular image of what Africans look like and use that to make fun of them. I can't put the blame solely on the Americans. Their imaginations are sparked by various sources, one being the media and another, history. From the media aspect, their idea of how Africans look came from some commercials they saw on TV. As a kid, I remember seeing the commercial where they ask you to donate even five dollars to help an African struggling from poverty. Most of the time, the kids look really skinny, are usually suffering from some kind of disease, and have flies all over their faces. I understand they are trying to create an effect on the audience to make them donate; however, I do feel it's a bit dramatic. The media made Africa seem like a place outside of plant earth with no culture, language, or customs. They made it seem as if Africa was solely a land of poverty and struggling humans. It was as if Africa was the only place on earth who beard such struggles. If you Google "Africans," you're not going to get the same kind of pretty and patriotic picture you would if you Google "Americans." This is the case in the year 2016.

It is not easier to be African now than it was when I came to America in 2003. The problem, to me, is a lack of resources. There are struggles all over the world, ranging in intensity. However, if one has the proper resources, one can overcome anything. Because there's a lack of resources in Africa, people tend to struggle there more than on the other continents, although not too many people see it like that. They interpret it in a way that would shame most Africans. The lie is prettier than the truth. Due to the image portrayed by the media, Americans already have such a negative perspective of Africans before they meet them. I find it funny, because one of the first things I learned in an American institution was not to judge a book by its cover.

From a historical perspective, did you know that in the twentieth century, the poorest white people felt comfortable knowing that blacks were under them? Similarly, due to years of oppression, black people felt comfort post-slavery, knowing that Africans were under them, in a way. I believe this is why continuous bullying and oppression are felt by Africans from black people. This didn't occur from nowhere. There is a lot of history behind it. However, it is no excuse for the way this made me and other Africans feel. During the time of slavery, most African Americans were not able to keep their names. They were forced to forget their history, their culture, and their names, which were taken away from them. Everyone knows the famous scene in *Roots* where the master beats the slave until he announces himself with the slave name that was given to him.

The same behaviors were shown by African Americans toward Africans. Not only was I called an African booty scratcher, but my family and I were accused of having AIDS. I remember kids wouldn't even play with me, because they suspected that if I touched them, they would be diagnosed with AIDS. They often questioned whether or not I wore clothes when I was in Ethiopia. In their heads, I walked around with a piece of cloth covering only my privates, barefoot, and lived in a hut. This was more theory that stemmed from the media. Granted, in some parts of Africa you might see a scenario like that, but not where I came from. To their surprise, I wore pants and a shirt, just like them, every day. After a while, I found their comments to be more amusing than anything.

I remember the Ebola outbreak in 2014. It was probably one of the worst times to be African. Ebola is a fatal disease. The virus is transmitted from wild monkeys and spreads to the human population through human-to-human transmission. Ebola stems from **West Africa**. I emphasize West Africa, because I want to continue to remind you that Africa is a continent. I remember that during the outbreak, I was scared as an African to cough in public. If I felt a sneeze or a cough come, I would have to excuse myself so I could cough or sneeze in private. That way, nobody could accuse me of having Ebola. During 2014, if you were African, you were no longer known as an African booty scratcher. Africans were thought to all have Ebola. Quite frankly, I would rather be known as an African booty scratcher than to have a fatal disease.

Things seemed to change slightly when I got to high school. I never got bullied, nor did any of my peers, much. Instead, we used to have these roast sessions. Roast sessions were basically what we called it when a group of people got together to make fun of one another or, in other words, roast each other. The roast sessions were never a way to put anyone down, but instead, they were something we did for fun, to see who had the best comebacks or who was the funniest. I must say I was pretty brutal with my comebacks and nobody really got on me much. My strategy was to say anything that they could possibly make fun of me for before they had the chance to say it. This way, they had to come at me from a different angle. I still do this in college. It works.

However, I remember how tough it was for me going to school when my sneakers were from Payless, so by the time I was in high school I was pretty "Americanized" in the sense that I wore name brands to avoid being picked on. I used to play on the school basketball team, and we would get name-brand sneakers for games and practices, which was a benefit. That didn't stop them from picking on me, though. In middle and high school, kids made fun of me for my haircuts. My mom did not want to pay twenty dollars every two weeks for me to get a cut, so she bought a set of clippers and had my older brother cut my hair. My brother was no barber, and you certainly could see that after he was done. I would go to school, and everybody would make fun of me, mostly because I didn't have a normal shape-up. I blame him to this day for my receding hairline. When people make fun of you, you start to feel bad about yourself and you don't even defend yourself, because you start to think, If I was them, I would be doing the same thing; maybe not to their faces, but in my head. I once read a quote from President Abraham Lincoln, who said, "Don't criticize them; they are just what we would be under the same circumstances." Just take a minute to really think about that.

I remember one summer I even went bald; it was the summer of 2006. My brother had gone to a camp for work, and my hair had grown tremendously. My mom decided to take things into her own hands. She got the clippers, plugged them into the wall, and started to work. The clippers had no oil, so they weren't working. There were a couple of patches on my head, and there was no way to revert that. Do you know what she did next? She shaved my hair. My head was as bright as the sun. My mom persuaded me that it looked good, so I was fine until I went to summer camp the next day. It was a brutal day for me. I could not wait to go back home. I went home crying, but my mother was not one for the tears. She told me I should have thicker skin and this was nothing for me to cry about. Surely, she had no clue how bad my day had been. It was fine, though. I was determined to not let her ever touch my hair again from that day on. When I was in Ethiopia, I remember I used to get my hair shaved to conserve money, so I didn't have to go to the barbershop often. In Ethiopia, nobody could make fun of me, because we were all bald. However, in America it was different. Kids went to the barber every week or every other week. A haircut was as important as what was on your feet.

High school had some of the funniest and most brutal moments of my life. I had a very dark-skinned friend and people always tried to make fun of him. It could happen anytime and anywhere. For example, the teacher would turn off the lights for a presentation and someone in class would be like, "Don't! It's hard enough to see Mohammed as it is." And he would have an epic comeback, like, "That's not what your moms said last night." The whole class would be oohing and ahhing. There were so many moments like this in high school, I often get flashbacks and just laugh in the middle of the day. Laughter is often the best medicine for anything. I've heard that people who laugh more live longer, so even in the harshest times, you have to remember to laugh and move on.

CHAPTER 3

Africa Is a Continent!

BELIEVE IT OR not, Africa is a continent. I repeat, Africa is a continent. Now I know for some people, it is a hard concept to grapple with. So here is a picture.. ☺:

See, I wasn't lying. Most people with common sense and an education probably know that Africa is a continent. However, for most Africans growing up in America, I know they know what I'm talking about. Most people refer to Africa as a country, not a continent. Not only is it a continent, it's the second largest continent in the world. Where does the idea of Africa being a country stem from? Of course, it's the media, journalists, and all the public figures that influence society to think of Africa as a country. Throughout this chapter I will give you various "Alternative facts" Presented to portray how different media channels and influencers continue to showcase Africa as a country. Simple mistakes such as when one visits a country in Africa and instead of saying the country they visited they say "I just came back visiting Africa."

One of the books that was suggested to me as a business student in college was *How to Win Friends and Influence People* by Dale Carnegie. What a phenomenal book it was. It really helped me change my way of thinking and had a tremendous effect on the way I interact with people. However, in chapter four, "An Easy Way to Become a Good Conversationalist," Carnegie wrote about attending a bridge party where he sat down with a woman and she told him about how she visited Africa. Not a country in Africa, just Africa. Carnegie stated how interesting it was and how he always wanted to go to Africa. He continued to say he envied her and asked her to tell him about "Africa." I want to curse, but because I want my younger siblings to read this book, I will refrain. It is this notion people have generalizing Africa as one big country that gives the wrong idea to people all around the world.

When people found out I was Ethiopian, those who knew that Ethiopia was in Africa would ask me what Africa was like. I would respond that I had no idea. They would look at me, confused, and say, "Aren't you from Africa?" For me, to answer the question "How is Africa?," I would have to visit the more than fifty countries on the continent. Outside of Ethiopia, I have not had an opportunity to visit any other African countries, therefore I can't tell you what "Africa" is like.

When President Obama went to Ethiopia in the summer of 2015, some reports stated that he would be traveling to Africa instead of saying he would be traveling to Ethiopia. In the short couple of days the president was in Ethiopia, he did not have time to visit any of the other countries in Africa. NBC News published an article stating, "Africa Ready for Obama Visit." Did "Africa," with over 1.2 billion people, start a GroupMe and say, "We are officially ready for Obama to come"? I think NBC needs to fire a few of its journalists and editors!

Here is another fact. Egypt is a part of Africa. Just because they speak Arabic and not "African," it does not separate them from being a part of Africa. There are many more factors as to why some Americans don't correlate Egypt with Africa. Could it simply boil down to the color of their skin? Since most people from Egypt have a lighter skin tone, most people would not correlate them as part of Africa. Since Africans are stereotyped as having a darker skin tone, if someone does not fit in that category, most would identify him or her as an African. Are the people from South Sudan, Nigeria, Ghana, or another region with darker color more African than their neighbors to the north, east, and south with lighter skin tone? Surely categorization based on race is unethical and ignores the continent's great diversity of nations, cultures, and ethnicities. What is the stereotypical view of what Americans imagine Africans look like? Really dark skin, with the typical African accent, which people get from watching movies. Most people know someone from Nigeria or Ghana, in my experience, and people tend to stereotype and think every country in Africa is like Nigeria or Ghana. However, it's not fair to judge how one should look based on assumptions or general classifications of ethnicity. It's like the assumption that Asians or white people all look alike.

Of course, some ethnicities have identifying characteristics regarding their background, but it doesn't hurt to ask before assuming. For example, with Ethiopians, skin tone, forehead, or even hair can help others classify them as being from Ethiopia. When I was growing up, everyone assumed I was Latino or from the Middle East, or from Egypt. Everyone assumed I was everything but Ethiopian. It got to the point that when somebody did identify me as Ethiopian, I would be ecstatic. If I had the bell that rings when you hit the lottery, that is what I would have played. I was intrigued to find out how they knew I was Ethiopian. Often they would say it was my face structure and my skin tone.

When I was growing up in New York, I was asked several ignorant questions when people found out I was African. "So, do you speak African? Do you eat African food? Did you grow up with lions? How did you get to school in Africa, did you ride an elephant? You're African? I thought you were from Ethiopia." Again, they did not correlate me as African because I didn't fit the typical stereotype of what they thought African meant. In the twenty-first century, with the rapid growth of technology and an abundance of resources that we have access to in America, people still remain ignorant about the "Dark Continent." I am still asked to this day, when people know I am from Africa, if I speak African. Unfortunately, I do not speak African, nor do the approximately 1.2 billion people who live in Africa. English is an official language in twenty-four African nations and taught at a high level in institutions across the continent. You know what I realized? Americans think they can put an "n" at the end of "Africa" and think it's a language, food, or custom. When I came to America, I didn't approach anyone asking if they spoke "American." They would laugh directly in my face!

Another funny thing: if you're from Africa or of African descent, you're not allowed to be hot. Well, at least in my experience. I remember during the summer days of elementary school, we would spend a period playing basketball or other recreational sports. When the period was over and we had to go to our next class, do you know how hot it would be in the classroom? Especially if you had a classroom without an air-conditioner. I could never say aloud I was hot. Why? Because that would be the only fuel my classmates would need to execute their ignorance. "Mike, why are you hot? Aren't you African!? Don't you live in the desert? This should be nothing new to you!" The fallacy that people have of Africa being a large desert is absolutely not correct; in fact, desert makes up only a small percentage. My classmates would get upset if I stated that I was hot. They didn't really understand that I came from a very small part of Africa, Ethiopia, where it isn't hot 365 days a year. Some days it was cold, but my classmates would never really believe me. The problem was, they never looked at me as an Ethiopian, mostly as an African. So never mind how it was where I came from, all they knew was that Africa was portrayed as extremely hot. If I stated that there were changes in weather there, that would get the same response as if I had said the tooth fairy existed. The most widely recognized spots for snow in Africa are ski resorts in Morocco, in the little nation of Lesotho, and in the southern mountains in South Africa. In a few nations with particularly high elevation, for example, Kenya, snow gathers on the highest points of the mountains. Indeed, even areas with Mediterranean atmospheres, such as Cairo, Egypt, can encounter snowfall; this was seen in 2013, when the Middle East got an exceptionally sudden snowstorm.

In respect to languages, in my country alone there are more than eighty languages! The main language is Amharic, which I speak fluently to this day. Other main languages people speak in Ethiopia are Tigrinya, Oromo, Gurage, Somali, and even Arabic. Thousands of languages are spoken on the African continent. Forgive us if we don't speak African, we haven't gotten around to it. Most likely because it doesn't exist.

During grade school and even college, teachers often stressed the idea that there is no such thing as a stupid question! I would like to challenge that idea. If you are in a place where you lack resources and are living in a cave, then by all means, ask all the stupid questions you want. Only then would I respect the notion of no stupid question. However, in a place where you can find a library anywhere you go, access free Wi-Fi in most areas, and have books all around you, don't tell me there's no such thing as a stupid question. Radio personality Charlamagne tha God often states, "Nobody cares about the truth if the lie is more entertaining." His theory is absolutely correct. I listen to him often, because he speaks nothing but the truth. For most Americans, it's thrilling for them to think I was raised around the cast of "The Lion King." You know, the funny part is, when I got older I stopped attempting to educate people about the diversity and culture of Africa. I would instead feed their figment of imagination and say stuff like, "At the age of seven, I killed my first lion." As ridiculous as it was for me to say that, the fact that they believed me, in my opinion, was worse. Of course, I would reiterate that I was only joking, but they would take what I said and run with it.

When I finally got them to believe there were actual people living in Africa, they would then ask if there were any white people. Well, are there any black people in Europe? During the 1870s and early 1900s, much of Africa were being colonized by seven European countries such as Britain, France, Germany, Belgium, Spain, Portugal, and Italy. When these European countries were on a mission to colonize, they made a few stops at different countries in Africa. In fact, by the early twentieth century, most parts of Africa were colonized by Europeans, except for Ethiopia and Liberia. Long after the colonization, white people did indeed stay over. So throughout Africa, you will certainly see white faces. ☺

Some Americans, and even people outside of America, have no clue what Africa is actually like, except for stereotypical rumors or their imagination. Movies like "The Lion King," "Madagascar," and others have portrayed Africa as a continent full of animals, undermining the 1.2 billion people who reside there. People see this stereotypical view and run with it. The notion of a giraffe running around and talking with monkeys and people assuming I grew up with a pet lion are simply ridiculous. People would joke around and ask me questions like "What was it like growing up with a pet lion?" It's like me asking an American how it was growing up with a pet bear! Granted, in small regions of Africa, it might be like that. It might be a place full of animals, like a zoo or something. However, the impression that the continent of Africa is made up of the cast of "The Lion King" is ridiculous. There are as many wild animals running through the cities in Africa as in cities in America. Which is very minimal if any! Africa is home to some of the most brilliant people and has an abundance of history. Africa is not just a place filled with animals. The first time I saw many animals people would assume roam around in Africa was at the

Bronx Zoo. When we arrived at the zoo, my friends stated that I must have felt right at home with all the animals around. Not only did they think I grew up with them, they thought I could speak to the animals. They would tell me to command the animals to move around.

The notion that people have of the way Africans communicate with one another, through clicking language, is unbelievable. In South Africa, there is a form of language that consists of clicks, called Xhosa. It does exist, but only in certain places in Africa, which, again, can't be categorized the same for everyone from Africa. Africa is no longer the "Dark Continent," it's home to some of the fastest growing economies in the world. The misconception can no longer be tolerated. If you took some time to do some research, you would become immensely educated. It's now the bright continent with so much potential. When the continent of Africa is given the right resources, there is nothing that's not achievable.

When I came to America, I had no clue what I was getting myself into. The only things I knew about America were what I heard from family, friends, and the media. The difference is that I sought to learn the culture, customs, and foods. I never generalized or put all Americans in one category. Everyone in America was different and looked different. And even if I did generalize everyone, it would be in a positive way. Such as: All Americans are successful. All Americans are nice people who want to help others. America is the land of the free, the brave, and equality. When people categorize Africa, they speak about the continent being full of disease, hunger, war, and poverty. When I came to the United States, I read d of books and asked tons of questions. What I realized about Americans is that they assume before they ask.

People used to ask me questions like whether I ate fufu or jollof rice, which some people eat in certain regions of Africa. I had no clue what fufu or jollof rice was until I was introduced to them by my friend from Nigeria. When Americans ask if I eat African food, they categorize it in three to five dishes. Meanwhile, there are thousands of cuisines in Africa. For example, in Ethiopia we eat injera, which is the main dish. Most Americans describe injera as a spongy bread or taco.

Different dishes go on top of the injera, and you use the injera to eat the dishes. I remember offering my friend some Ethiopian food, and I brought the food in front of him. He sat and stared at it for a couple of minutes. I asked him what was wrong. He said he was waiting for the fork. I explained that Ethiopian food is eaten with your hand. Don't get me wrong, we have tons of food that you can use a fork and knife for. But most food is eaten with your hand. It's quite delicious, I must say! However, it's not surprising to find typical American dishes and restaurants in certain regions of Africa. Places such as McDonald's, KFC, and many others. There are places one can go to find some of the best steakhouses, pizza, and even seafood.

When I came to America and started to learn about some of the ridiculous stereotypes of Africa, I was shocked. Everything they assumed was news to me. I had to do research, because everybody expected everyone from Africa to be alike, and when I said I didn't do certain things stereotypical of many Africans, I was accused of being a "fake African." People around me continued to ignore the great diversity of Africa. Here is a relationship that might be easier to connect to: it's similar to the idea of African Americans being uneducated, disrespectful, and aggressive. If someone doesn't fall into that category, it's like me saying he is a fake African American. This isn't like a knock-off handbag or merchandise. In respect to one's culture, you can't ignore the abundant diversity. It seems easier for people to say you're fake if you don't fit the typical stereotype they have in their head.

At the 2014 Olympics, Delta Air Lines made a crucial mistake when congratulating the US soccer team for a win against Ghana. The mistake was not that the company wished the US team "congratulations," but it used a giraffe to represent Ghana as one of the many nations in Africa. Now, most people reading this are probably wondering what is wrong with that. The problem is that there are, in fact, no wild giraffes in Ghana. It's bad enough when the media works tirelessly to portray Africa as a big zoo filled with poverty and war. However, when we have a major company like Delta exhibiting such behavior, it says very little about the ethics of the company and its awareness of the other parts of the world. The picture of the giraffe is said to be from Getty Images, and it's of the Masai Mara National Reserve in Kenya, one of the many nations in Africa. To the company's credit, Delta Air Lines apologized. If it wasn't for the people who were above the stereotypes of Africa, Delta would never have discovered what it had done wrong. What the company did was to heighten awareness of a stereotype that is perpetuated in society and the media. There are certainly giraffes, lions, and all kinds of exciting wild animals in Africa. Just as there are emerging cities with beautiful landscapes and great innovation happening in Africa. We have to stop looking at Africa as a country; otherwise, we are going to bring up another generation of uninformed and ignorant individuals. It's believed that one of the first forms of humanity began in Ethiopia, a place in Africa. It's unfair to discredit all these nations with their rich history and just put them under the umbrella of "Africa." If you want to see the bones of the first presumed human, you have to go to Ethiopia. Africa's diversity in its history and people is something that shouldn't go unnoticed and be categorized.

Have you ever seen the meme "Every 60 seconds in Africa a minute passes"? If you haven't, please go look at the endless memes on Google to go along with this chapter.

This is a viral meme that was floating around. What does it mean? Well, for one, even in Africa a minute equals sixty seconds. The meme is supposed to be funny if analyzed correctly. There have been tons of videos saying "an African child will die every minute (or every day) without your donation." I have no problem with those commercials, because most of the organizations are truly trying to help people. However, the way that people see those videos and run with them is what upsets me. They will see a video like that and associate Africa only with starving children and a high rate of poverty. I remember when growing up, sometimes kids would make fun of me and say something like, "For a few pennies a day, we can help Michael's family." The way I felt when people said things like that to me is inexpressible. It's like saving money for a long period of time to buy something and losing the money the day before. That hurt and anger is the same way I felt when kids used those Sunday commercials to make fun of me.

The reason this meme went viral is that it sheds light on the terrible things that happen in Africa, just like in any other place in the world. People only associate poverty, hunger, and diseases with Africa. However, these tragedies happen in America as well. America is perceived to be this perfect place, which is simply not true. Just like any other place in the world, America has its share of poverty, disease, and hunger. Feedamerica.org reported that 43.1 million Americans are in poverty. These are statistics that can be seen in real life at homeless shelters and churches that donate food and shelter to millions of Americans. If we open our eyes, we can really see what's going on in the world. Sure, Africa might have double or triple the numbers that America has in regard to poverty and hunger, but mostly because Africa has a lot more people in each nation and because of the lack of resources for most families.

Africa faces misconceptions about what it truly is. Mostly, Africa's huge diversity is ignored and often categorized into specific sections. Often, Africa is misconstrued as a country, and people don't see all the nations but rather a generalization of what they assume Africa is. For example, when people go on vacation, they usually name a specific place they are going to. However, when someone goes to a specific place in Africa, the first instinct is not to say he or she is going to Kenya, Ethiopia, Ghana, etc., but he or she would simply state that he or she is going to Africa.

During the 2016 presidential election, there was a division in America. Most Americans did not view Trump's ideals as ethical. The United States of America was a place that was supposed to represent everyone and allow equal freedom in respect to race, sex, and religion. Most people and especially African-Americans were sick of his ideals and threatened to leave America. Do you know where they were going to go? Everyone said they were going back to their roots, back to Africa. I saw it circulating on social media every day. I was getting frustrated seeing this. First of all, where in Africa are you going? Second of all, you don't even have a passport! There is no country named Africa on the map. I know some of my friends were saying that, and they haven't left their neighborhood all their lives. Let's start with visiting outside of your block before you travel thousands of miles to a place you have no clue about. They didn't even give us the benefit that planes fly to countries in Africa. The memes just said, "I'm taking the first boat back to Africa." I know it was meant to be funny, but deep down I knew that most people who were posting it really thought they could take a boat to Africa. As humans, we need to be open to the idea that things are more than what we assume them to be. Often we have our own ideas and shut down any objection that tells us otherwise. Remember to be open-minded. Oh, and **Africa is a continent, not a country.**

CHAPTER 4

⚜

What Are Thooooooose?

HAVE YOU EVER heard that phrase that went viral, "What are thoseee?" There are tons of videos all over social media platforms with an individual pointing at knock-off brand sneakers and screaming "What are those?!" If you have never seen it, I encourage you to Google it so you have a sense of what I am talking about. There have been several articles based on this viral saying, such as in *The Washington Post*. Of course, you will find tons of memes on the Internet and many social media platforms about the phrase. I am so happy this phrase came out now that I am a bit more "Americanized" and wear brand-name sneakers. That's sounds selfish, doesn't it? I feel like I reached the capability of getting bullied, if that is a thing. However, this is important for all the kids who continue to get bullied for not conforming. There is a culture in America that I have noticed where people who don't follow along with what is trending will often get bullied for being different. This chapter is not going to be confined to only sneakers or clothes. Kids who seek to be different are often targets for bullies. I remember during grade school when the teacher would give the students their grades on an exam. If most of the class failed and you had the highest grade, you were going to be the joke of the day. Did you cheat? You're a teacher's pet! No one praised you for getting a good grade. No one assumed that the reason for the good grade was that you studied and paid attention in class. Or you had a strict parent who would not allow you to come home with anything but an A.

After a while, I started lying. If I had a high grade and the people in my class failed, and they asked me what I got, I would straight-up lie. If they got a 58, I got a 54. If they got 68, I got 63, and so on. I noticed that the lower the grade I had, the cooler my peers perceived me. Lord knows that if I had ever presented my mother with such grades, she would not be very fond of them, but I found a way to please my mother by excelling in school and lied to my peers to get through the school year. I would shake hands and laugh like it was nothing, while I secretly folded up that 95 percent grade I got and threw it in my book bag before anyone saw it. When I was growing up in Ethiopia, the kids who got low grades were often punished. There was a competitive spirit in the classroom to see who would get the highest grade. The kid with the lowest grade would get made fun of, and would be punished by the instructor. The culture was different when I was growing up in America. But just like anything else, I learned to live and adapt.

I found myself conforming more and more to fit in as an African growing up in America. When you grow up with such a low level of confidence like I did, you just try to fit in among everyone else. I got tired of standing out. Little did I know that standing out was what was going to make me successful.

I knew I was a little different from all of my peers. I knew I had a purpose for coming to America. I had several jobs in college, and one of them was working in a retail store. It was one of the jobs I loved and hated the most. I loved it because of the interaction I had with the customers. However, I hated it because I faced such challenges as trying to find what rack the clothes went in when customers left them in the dressing room. I often just shoved the clothes in places where I thought they fit. Throughout my life, I have continued to learn and adapt. So just like the cloths in the dressing room I shoved in a rack where I thought resembled, I kind of did the same thing with my life. I changed the rack I was in depending on the environment, behavior or culture that was before me.

When I was in school, I hated dress-down day. All of my peers would be excited when we had dress-down days. I, on the other hand, didn't like it much, not because I didn't have clothes outside of my uniform, but because I didn't have clothes that would be accepted by my peers. So when my classmates came to school wearing True Religion jeans with the latest Jordans, I came in with some regular jeans my mom bought from Conway, a T-shirt, and my all-white Shaquille O'Neal sneakers that resembled the Air Force 1s. I thought I was looking fly, but not to my peers. If the phrase "what are those?" was a thing when I was younger, I would have been the main target. One time, I decided to go to dress-down day wearing a suit. I didn't own a lot of casual clothing; my mom often dressed me as a professional. I'd go to the playground with slacks and a button-down. So when we had dress-down day, I decided to wear the suit. I remember it like it was yesterday. It was an all-brown suit, with polished black shoes. I was more dressed up than the teacher. I thought I would get a better response than my previous outfit. Boy, was I wrong! My peers stared at me and asked if I was about to give the word. "Mike always trying to be white." "Are you the substitute teacher or what?" The phrase that stuck out to me was "Mike always trying to be white." Dressing up and having success were apparently correlated with being white.

I'm in college and I still get asked questions every time I dress up. I remember watching the movie "Dope," and there was a line that stuck out for me: "Why do I want to attend Harvard? If I was white, would you even have to ask me the question?" When people ask me why I'm always dressed up, I sarcastically ask, "If I was white, would you ask me the same question?" I didn't understand why people associated success with race. I found it mind-boggling, because there were tons of successful people of all races, not only white. It would be ignorant to ignore the fact that the history of America portrays a land of racism and discrimination, only allowing whites opportunities for education, jobs, and growth. However, in the twentieth and twenty-first centuries, America has come far. Of course, there is still racism and discrimination; we saw how apparent it is from the Trump campaign. However, I do believe that if you are willing to put the work in, anyone can be successful. My mindset for how I dressed was that I didn't dress for the job I had, I dressed for the job I wanted. I didn't let race dictate my success; success was my only choice. The main reason I came to America was to be given the resources to be successful; it was up to me to obtain the success I wanted. Everything I've ever gotten was earned.

America is certainly not where it should be, but it's far from where it was. I feel like it's no longer the system holding people back from success, but people's own mindset. Society is so stuck on how things were that people fail to see where they could be if they used their resources to achieve what they wanted. That was one of the first occurrences with cultural appropriation. Cultural appropriation is defined in the Urban Dictionary as "the ridiculous notion that being of a different culture or race (especially white) means that you are not allowed to adopt things from other cultures. This does nothing but support segregation and hinders progress in the world. All it serves to do is to promote segregation and racism." My friend Mohammed had it worse, though. He came to school wearing his traditional dashiki from Ghana, and the class looked at him in disgust. A dashiki is colorful apparel for men and women, widely worn in West Africa and in other parts of Africa. However, here was my friend showing his diversity and culture in America, but instead of being glorified, he was insulted. Fast-forward to the present time, and the dashiki is one of the most quickly emerging fashions in America. It has been worn by megastars like Beyoncé, Rihanna, and many others. Now you see individuals of both sexes and from different cultures walking around with dashikis and making a fashion statement. However, for many Africans, this is a part of their culture, when not too long ago they were ridiculed for wearing apparel that was not accepted in America and thought to be different. After megastars started wearing dashikis, many people gave it a stamp of approval.

Now, I am not being a hypocrite and saying that African -Americans, and other races should not be allowed to wear dashikis because they did not come directly from a place in Africa. What I am saying is, how can society harass and make fun of Africans for wearing dashikis and then turn around and claim them as an emerging trend and label them acceptable? However, society evolved and people started wearing them to show their

"Africanism," and some used them make a profit. Before, anyone who wore a dashiki would be ridiculed; we must learn our history. For most Africans who wear dashikis, it's not at all about the dashiki, but about embracing their culture, showcasing their pride and their diversity. If society labeled the dashiki "out of style," it would never go out of style for most Africans. That dashiki is a part of who they are, and no matter what happens, they will continue to embrace and wear their dashiki.

Often individuals are ridiculed for being different and standing out, although sometimes what they are ridiculed for wearing will become a trend. It will become fashionable in the future. Conforming is easier than trying to be different. When one conforms, he or she often won't be accepted. Why do you think I got bullied so much? Now, I'm not saying I was this brave kid who refused to conform. No matter how strong you are, you are bound to conform. It's not for the heck of it, either; it's about survival and a life of ease.

Why I stopped wearing my sneakers my mom bought at Payless was not because they were not comfortable, too big, or something like that. It was simply because I did not want to be the guy everyone pointed at and screamed, "What are those?" I had to conform to the brand-name sneakers because it finally got to me. It was affecting my day-to-day life. I was so insecure about what I had on that it affected my academic and social life. I was constantly thinking about what they were thinking about. The kids emphasized what was on the outside rather than what was on the inside. Think about the coolest kid in high school. The coolest kid most of the time was the badass who had every new sneaker that came out and all the brand names. That was the guy most girls were attracted to. I feel like the phrase "What are those?" just puts more emphasis on how much Americans emphasize materialism. You would never make fun of a kid for wearing Louis Vuitton unless it was fake. Nevertheless, why would somebody even wear fake brands? Because of the need to fit in.

Wearing a brand is another form of slavery, in my opinion. It enslaves people into thinking these brands are what is important and defines what kind of person they are. Historically speaking, branding was a tool of ownership. Branding took place with both humans and animals. In the modern day it's different. For example, a student who graduates from Yale, Harvard, or any other Ivy League institution is branded to be the best of the best compared to students graduating from non–Ivy League schools. Or how we brand convicted felons as being a dishonor to society. This same kind of branding has been manufactured with big name brands. Society has unfortunately fallen for the branding that has been implemented. People put more emphasis on what they wear instead of who they are as a person. Materialism has so much power that just a name on accessories can give us a world of encouragement and motivation. You walk differently when you've got on red-bottomed Christian Louboutin heels versus regular heels. I was a victim too; I had a little bounce when I had popular brand-name shoes versus shoes from Payless. People like to feel good, they love the attention they get when they wear brand names. Think about how many compliments you get when you have the Louis bag or the MK watch. These brand names make you feel like you're something. They give enough power to make little Mohammed or Michael feel inhuman because he cannot afford the brand name you have. The messed-up part was that the people who often had these brand names were broke themselves! They would spend their last dollar for a brand name and have no money for lunch. I saw this every day in high school: the kid with all the coolest gear didn't have a dollar for an Arizona beverage. We should focus less on what's on the outside and appreciate people for the knowledge they bring to elevate our society. Look at Warren Buffett, one of the richest men on earth. A kid from Harlem will have on triple the cost of apparel than what that billionaire has on, if you compare them side-by-side.

You know what I blame for people being so materialistic? The media, of course, and I specifically blame the hip-hop and rap game. As kids, we wanted to be everything they were: we wanted to live their lifestyle and wear what they wore. We listened to the lyrics they wrote and tried to match our lives with theirs. The problem was that we were a couple of million dollars away from living the luxury lifestyle they had.

Let's look at sneakers to help us paint a more vivid picture. How many kids have died in the US because of some Jordans? I saw a clip on the news where a kid was shot dead over some sneakers. This shows you that people are willing to live a lifestyle that they can't necessarily afford by any means. With lyrics glorifying success with immense money, cars, and sneakers, it creates an illusion for people listening to that context of what success truly is. Of course, there has been a stand against this with the emergence of stars like J. Cole, Kendrick Lamar, Drake, etc., rapping about stuff that normal people can relate to, such as the violence that happens in society, standing against the government, and motivating people to go after their dreams with their lyrics by teaching from their experience to help others.

CHAPTER 5

#GrowingupAfrican?

How to be an African parent:

1. Shout.
2. Blame everyone at home but yourself.
3. Never apologize to your kids.
4. Shout.
5. Keep shouting.

African career options:

1. Doctor
2. Lawyer
3. Engineer
4. Disgrace to the family

Grading system in an African house:

A: Average
B: Below average
C: Can't eat dinner
D: Don't come home
E: Find a new family

EVERYTIME YOU COMPLAIN ABOUT SOMETHING YOUR PARENTS GIVE YOU THE INFAMOUS "WHEN I WAS YOUR AGE" SPEECH.

WHY DID I put a question mark next to the chapter title? The reason is that I don't want to sound like a hypocrite. Throughout the previous chapter, I talked about society generalizing people from Africa. However, in this chapter, I will be doing a lot of generalization. Although Africa is a place full of diversity and different cultures, I have learned that most Africans in my generation have had the same experiences growing up. Growing up African is probably one of the most difficult things ever. The struggle is very real! If you ever want to get a good laugh, search #growingupafrican.

When I was in Ethiopia, I didn't see a vast difference in how my peers and I were raised. We had similar experiences. Our parents expected a lot from us, we got beaten if we messed up, education was stressed, and respect and discipline were a must! However, when I came to America, it was a different ball game. There was a complete difference in how I was raised and how my friends were raised. Growing up, I had no curfew. That didn't mean I could stay out as long as I wanted and come home as I pleased; because you are African, you know there will be great repercussions for that kind of behavior. I had no curfew because I knew that after school I had to go straight home. Think about it like a ticking bomb: if you don't cut the proper wire before the hour is up, it will blow up. Now use that perspective in regard to African parents.

Among all African cultures, the two things that were similar across the board, in my opinion, were the level of discipline and the manners that were stressed upon us. Our parents raised us in a way that when we were outside of the home, we still carried the discipline that was taught to us, which meant to excel in school and respect everyone. Growing up in an African home, you had a code of ethics. Such as never use your left hand for anything; you might as well not even have it, because you are instructed to do everything with your right hand. When someone older comes in the room, you have to instantly stand up to show respect. You should never look at somebody older in the eye, because that is sign of disrespect. But it is the opposite in American culture; it is a sign of respect to look somebody in the eye. Such ethics plus a lot more are common among most African countries. It was amazing to me the similarities I shared with my different African friends.

Here are the top ten things that every African growing up had in common:

1. **Turning eighteen meant absolutely nothing!**
2. **There was no such thing as a sleepover.**
3. **Nothing we did was ever good enough.**
4. **Our parents never bought us anything expensive that didn't have to do with school.**
5. **If your teacher called your parents, it was over for you!**
6. **You couldn't talk about sex or see it on TV, and if you did, it was very awkward.**
7. **Your parents were straight-A students.**
8. **You had no options when it came to food; you ate what was in the fridge and were grateful.**
9. **You were threatened to get sent back to your country by your parents.**
10. **You were constantly compared to friends and children of your parents' friends.**

Now let's break this down further so you can really understand the struggle. The memes that you see on social media about growing up African are funny, but for most Africans, it's our life.

1. Turning eighteen meant absolutely nothing!

When I turned eighteen, I was a senior in high school. In America, when you turn eighteen, you're grown. Most American parents would consider you to be an adult. You have the opportunity to move out of your parents' house and be on your own, if you want. Not in an African household. You were not grown until you graduated from college and got your master's and PhD, as well as got married and had kids; then maybe your parents might consider you an adult. In high school, my friends would invite me to go to the movies, a party, or a get-together. I would try to find any excuse in the book to get out of the invitation without making it seem like it was because of my parents. There were some things I didn't waste my time asking my parents about, because I knew they would look at me in disgust if I mustered the courage to even ask them. I would come up with excuses, such as, "Oh sorry, I've already got plans," or, "My bad, I'm going away this weekend, so I can't come." Meanwhile, I would be at my house doing nothing, probably reading a book, looking outside the window, watching people have fun. I would post fake stuff on Facebook like "Virginia lit," (Which basically meant it was a fun and exciting place)so my friends would believe that I really was away. After a while, people stopped bothering to ask me. They knew I would come up with some excuse not to go. They didn't really understand that at the age of eighteen, I had to call my mom to do anything outside of my academics. My friends would be like, "Aren't you eighteen? Why are you always calling your mom for things?" Eighteen in an African household was nothing more than the number that comes after seventeen.

It was never that African parents were trying to oppress us and not let us have fun. Although at the time I wished I did have American parents; I thought my life would be much better. However, it was that African parents wanted nothing but the best for their kids. They wanted to make sure that when you left their house, you would have the ability to handle yourself in the real world. In an African household, being an adult was not about being of age to drink and stay out as long as you wanted. It was about being capable of not only helping yourself but helping your parents and family back home.

2. There was no such thing as a sleepover!

One of my best friends in high school would often invite me to his house. Sometimes I would go to his house to play video games for an hour or two, and then immediately rush home. When I was at his house, I was never mentally at his house. My mind would be racing with what excuse I was going to tell my mom for coming home so late. Meanwhile, it was only 5:00 p.m. It was still pretty early, and the sun was still high in the sky. One day, my friend asked me to sleep over at his house, that way we could play the new 2K game the whole weekend. Now, if you are African, you know there was no way on earth your parents would have allowed this. If you dared to ask such a question, they would just say something along the lines of "Did I bring you to this country to sleep over at somebody's house? Do you think I worked this hard to bring you here just to go to sleep at somebody else's house? So you don't have a bed in this house and a roof over your head?" They would then get mad that you had the audacity to ask them such a foolish question. They would insist that you get out of their face quickly and go read or clean something! The only time they might allow you to sleep over at someone else's house was if it was a direct family member. It was never getting hit by my mom that would hurt me, it was the words she said that hurt.

My parents didn't want me to sleep over at someone else's house, not because they were trying to be mean parents and give their children no freedom (although this might have been true for some), it was that they didn't trust anybody to take care of me and be certain of my safety. They didn't want me to leave the house and come back with unhealthy behaviors such as smoking and drinking. African parents loved watching the news. The news would be nothing but terrifying. If they heard that someone was hit by a car in a certain area, African parents would ban you from walking in that area. Although they lacked the ability to show affection, I know that they loved us to death. They would do anything to ensure our health and safety, and if that meant isolating us from the whole world, so be it.

3. Nothing we did was ever good enough.

It was hard for me to watch my friends grow up with the abundance of freedom they had. I always thought that if I had American parents, they would really cherish me. Often, my friends' parents would tell me they wished their son was more like me. I was very disciplined, I had respect for everybody I met. I excelled in school, and I won every academic award possible. If I achieved what I had with most American parents, they would have been thrilled with all of my achievements. They would have spoiled me to death. My friends at the time were spoiled, making half the progress I had. My friends would get every new pair of sneakers and all the new technological devices that came out. When a new video game system came out, they all had it. On the other hand, I could not relate. I watched YouTube videos of the new systems so I could learn about all the features. When my friends in school would talk about the new game system, I was able to join the conversation. YouTube was the best thing that happened to me. I no longer had to be out of the conversation. I would learn everything about anything new that my friends were getting to the point where I believed that I had it too. The mind is a really powerful thing. It got to a point where I was making fun of people who didn't have the latest things. How ironic. When I got good grades, cleaned the house, or achieved anything, my parents really didn't make a big deal of it. Well, at least to my face; they would tell everyone on their phone contact list. They made us feel like what we were doing was never enough. You could win an award, and instead of congratulating you, they would ask how many people had applied.

When we couldn't make our parents happy, there were two things that we could do. Either we would do everything possible to excel at such a level that they had no choice but to praise us, or we would conclude that there was nothing we could do to make them happy and eventually give up. However, my parents' reactions encouraged me to continue to progress and elevate to a level that they had no choice but to express how proud of me they were. Sometimes I would get a hug, or an "I love you." A happy African mother means a happy home. The thing that made African parents happiest was the success of their children. I worked hard every day to make sure that my mom was proud of me, because my success meant that she would be happy, and her happiness was very important to me.

4. Our parents never bought us anything expensive that didn't have to do with school.

The first day of school, my friends always came with the newest Jordans. There was no way I would be able to afford two-hundred-dollar sneakers. There was no way I would even ask my mother to buy them for me. The first time I got expensive sneakers was when I joined the basketball team. The whole team got LeBrons. I was hyped! I wore those sneakers every day. My teammates only wore them during basketball practice. On the other hand, I wore them for class, basketball practice, basketball games, and all sorts of occasions. I wore those sneakers to death. Most of my peers were very materialistic; there was no way I could ever compete with them. Growing up, I was very fortunate. I grew up having all the necessities I ever needed. If I ever needed anything for school, my parent would never hesitate to get it. However, for any extracurricular activities, my mom would not be with it! "Why do I have to pay ten dollars for you to go to the Bronx Zoo again? You just went last year." Africans are very conservative. It wasn't because they didn't have the money to buy us whatever we needed, but because they thought there were better ways they could spend their money. They were very responsible and wanted to allocate their funds wisely. Every penny that they spent was accounted for, literally. Even when we got them to agree to buy us what we wanted, they would try to find the cheapest option. Or try to convince us why we didn't need it now and should wait until later. They knew that if we waited, there was a chance we wouldn't ask again, or we would end up forgetting about it. Clever! Not only would they opt out of buying something expensive, we would get in trouble if we bought it ourselves. They would get really upset and would say things like, "So you're grown now, huh? You want to pay for the rent now, Mr. Money Man?"

They really wanted us to know the value of money. They didn't want us to grow up too fast. They believed everything had its time: expensive sneakers, technology, or whatever it was. They didn't want to expose us to too many things at once and make us dependent on materialistic items. They didn't want our self-esteem and pride to rise from what was on the outside; rather, they wanted people to judge us based on what was within. The publicity constantly on TV of all the child stars in America getting in trouble with the law was our parents' prime example of why they did what they did. As soon as it came on the news, they would call us over and wouldn't even say anything. They would just want us to look at the news and praise them for how they were raising us.

5. If your teacher called your parents, it was over for you!

So far from reading this book, you might conclude that I'm kind of a funny guy. However, being funny often had repercussions for me. I used to always crack jokes with my friends, and often I was responsible for being the stand-up comedian in class. Although many teachers were not too fond of this and couldn't care less about my jokes. They wanted their authority respected and didn't want to hear a single thing out of our mouths unless we were instructed to speak. When the teacher threatened to call my friends' parents, they would just laugh or say funny remarks like, "Tell them I said hi." However, I would be terrified. When my teachers told me that they would call my mom, I would beg them not to. When a teacher threatened to call your parents, it was like the doctor diagnosing you with a major disease. Well, maybe it wasn't that drastic, but the initial feeling I got was almost identical. I would try to be the best-behaved student for the rest of the day. Unfortunately, there were times that my plea did not work and the teachers called home. They had no idea what kind of bomb they had just set off. I would sit in class contemplating suicide or running away, but I knew my mom would still beat me if I did either. Going home the day my teacher called my mom was the scariest thing ever. I would rush home, clean everything in the house, and try to go to bed early, around 7:00 p.m., before my mom got back from work. That never worked, because as soon as my mom got home, it was over. No matter what I was in the middle of doing when she came in, I was about to get smacked for misbehaving in school. She would insist that I apologize to my teacher, but I would go to school the next day with such hate in my heart for the teacher calling my mother and getting me in trouble. When my mom asked if I apologized, I would quickly respond, "That was the first thing I did when I got to school." Meanwhile, I went the whole day without uttering a word in class.

I am so glad that I had someone hold me accountable for everything I did. When I look back at my life now, compared to my peers who had no accountability, I can see the difference. All the yelling and beatings that I received shaped me into being the man I am today. I know that no matter what I do, I must think ahead to what I will have to face, whether it is positive or not. With that being said, thank you to all the teachers who called my mother. Although I disliked you then, nevertheless, I see now what you were aiming to do. School was the number-one priority for African parents, and any foolish behavior that occurred in school other than learning was not going to be tolerated.

6. You couldn't talk about sex or see it on TV, and if you did, it was very awkward.

Sex was taboo in an African household. It was almost like a curse word; you couldn't say it, watch it, or even think about doing it. African parents rarely brought it up. If you were watching anything other than the news with your parents and a sex scene came up, you knew you had to start looking the other way or excuse yourself to go to the bathroom. I know that as you read that, you're thinking it's normal for a child to do that. However, in an African household, a child is defined as someone with African parents who doesn't have a college degree, a wife, or kids. Growing up, you were not allowed to have a girlfriend or boyfriend; your primary focus was school. When my friend broke up with his fifth girlfriend, all I could think was that I didn't even have one girlfriend yet. When girls started liking me, I had to find a way for them to not like me anymore, because there was no way any relationship was going to take place between us.

I mean, now that I'm older, I guess our parents were trying to avoid teenage pregnancy. They wanted us to focus on school and not have anything to deter us from having great academic achievements. The only girlfriend/boyfriend we were going to have was our academics.

7. Your parents were straight-A students.

African parents painted themselves to be the smartest people to ever bless the earth. Every time they talked about their experience in school, they talked about how they were child prodigies. How they got As on all the exams, and if it was possible for them to get a higher grade, that's probably what they would have gotten. They would tell stories about how they were so smart that the teacher would look to them to teach the class or get answers. When you got your grades back from school, if they were lower than an A or A-minus, they would go on about how bad a student you were. They wouldn't understand why there was any reason you shouldn't get straight As, which I found contradictory, because African kids had a lot of responsibilities, especially if they had siblings. Your parents depended on you for a lot of help.

I know that my parents weren't straight-A students, because I'm sure they got a B or a B-minus sometimes. However, they told us they had nothing less than an A! Why? Because they had to set the bar so high that you had no choice but to try to achieve that success. As a child, your parents would not be satisfied with anything short of an A. This paved the way for me, and now that I'm in college, I don't aim for anything short of an A. In college, we have a dean's list and a principal's list. For the dean's list, you need to have at least a 3.2 GPA for the semester, and for the president list a 3.7 GPA. Every semester, I wanted to make the president list. My friends have a motto: "Cs get degrees." But in my culture, Cs gets beatings. My goal every semester is to make the 4.0 club. The training and leadership that my mom instilled in me don't let me be average. When I get a 3.6 GPA, I am mad rather than excited. I am not satisfied with anything less than a 4.0. I have not achieved this goal yet, although I've come close lots of times. Good is the enemy of great! My friends would be thrilled with my grade, because "good" is good enough for them. The reason that people don't try to reach the next level is because average is easy. Being good is easy; it doesn't require a lot of work from you. However, when you have African parents who worked to give you everything they had so that you could be successful, good is not an option. The only option is to be great and continue to reach unthinkable milestones.

8. You had no options when it came to food; you ate what was in the fridge and were grateful.

You know when you come home from school or work hungry, and you open the fridge and there's a ton of food inside, but instead you see an empty fridge, because there is nothing appealing to you? If you're African, you did not have that option of seeing an empty fridge when there was actually food in there. If you dared to even utter such foolishness to your parents about not having food in the fridge, you would never have heard the end of it. Not only would you get slapped before you finished the sentence, you would get a full three-hour lecture. You would hear about all the kids around the world who didn't have what you had. You would hear about how you were such an ungrateful child and how spoiled you were.

Unlike me, my little sister was born in America. It's one thing to come from Africa and try to grow up in America. However, to be born in America and grow up African was tough as well. My sister would come home from school, and when we served her dinner, she would refuse to eat it or complain about having eaten the same thing the day before. I would be mad at her for saying that because of the way I was raised. However, I left it to my mom to handle that statement. She talked to her the same way she would talk to me, and my sister and I are fourteen years apart. She learned a valuable lesson that day, and since then she is content with whatever we give her. Even when we might be driving by a McDonald's after going to church, she'll say, "Let's go get a Happy Meal, Mom," and my mom will say, "There is rice in the house!"

Our parents were trying to teach us the importance of being grateful for what we had. The lesson was bigger than the food; it was about having gratitude and knowing where you came from and never forgetting that. Even if you came from a place of privilege, they wanted us to know about people who were less fortunate and didn't have what we had. Our parents trained us to be thankful for everything we had, because somewhere out there was a kid wishing they were in the same predicament as us!

9. You were threatened to get sent back to your country by your parents.

If we got in trouble at school, if we were not up to par with their high standards of academics, or anything that went against their rules, they threatened to send us back to our home country. I felt like an Amazon package! At any second I could be sent back if I (the product) was not up their expectations. Most of the time when they threatened us, we all knew that they were probably joking, but we didn't want to take that risk. So, every time we got threatened with that notion, we would try to get our act together as quickly as possible. It was nothing against going back to our countries in Africa; it was just that we were comfortable here. We didn't really want to start over and not have the same opportunities and privileges that we had in America. I had the opportunity to go back to Ethiopia in the summer of 2015. I was excited to go back, but I thought it was a setup and I wouldn't be able to come back to America. I made sure to look at my ticket and confirm it was a two-way flight.

Looking back at it now, I don't think they would ever really have sent us back for anything. Unless it was something major that we messed up, then they might have sent us back express!

10. You were constantly compared to friends and children of your parents' friends.

African parents love comparing their kids to someone else's. You could have achieved something great, like winning a $10,000 scholarship for school, but if your parents knew someone who got a full scholarship, that's all you would hear about. African parents were in competition with each other when it came to their kids. "Your son made the newspaper, that's good, but my son was on television." It was like a battle of whose kids were the most successful. That's why they pressured us to be successful, so they could show off to their friends. African parents love to display their kids' talent. When I was younger, I played the trumpet and clarinet, and every time we had people over at the house, my mom would make me play. Other times, though, when I would be trying to practice, it would be, "What good is it to play an instrument? Are you going to play music for your career?" The funny part about African parents was that as much as they bragged about us to family and friends, they would talk about how terrible we were to our face, but to their friends we were gold. It was a rare occurrence when they would truly tell you that they were proud of you. I think the reason they didn't tell us as often as we liked was that they didn't want us to have a big head. They were trying to make us feel average even when we did excellent work so that we could continue to strive to achieve greatness.

Not only did we have to meet their high standards, but we had to be able to keep up with their friends' kids' successes. The result was that it made us competitive; at least it did for me. I wanted to be first in whatever I did. I wanted to have the highest grade, highest awards, etc. It was at a point that even if I achieved great success but it was second or third place, I would still be disappointed. Everything I did I took as a competition. I was competing with everyone around me and I strived to be number one. Even when it came to a simple game of Uno, best believe I was playing to win. I hate when people play to have fun or declare it's just a game. People who walk around with that mindset are mediocre people who do not strive to win at anything they do in life. That might be harsh, and I'm sorry if you feel that way after reading that. But my mindset in life is that if you're not playing to win, you're playing to lose.

Growing up in America was definitely tough, like I said. However, I know for sure that growing up in Africa would have been much tougher. However, don't for a second think that I couldn't have been successful if I had grown up in Ethiopia, because I would've been. Moreover, coming to America tripled my chances of being successful because of the abundant resources that were there for me. Our parents brought us to America to afford us all the opportunities they did not have. If there is a common thing that all African parents do, it's talking about what they would have been doing when they were our age. They would be like, "If I was you, I would have been a doctor already!" How?! First of all, I was only sixteen in high school, and you need to go through years of medical school to become a doctor. But for Africans parents, they felt like there was nothing they couldn't do; they were optimistic like no other. Often they knew they were bullshitting. Because they had to keep us on our feet, they would say anything. Or they would say how much more they would have been doing at our age if they had been given the same opportunities that were given to us. Yet they failed to realize that if they were growing up at our age in America, they would be in the same predicament that we were in. They pictured themselves as they were at our age. However, they didn't really understand how tough it was growing up in a culture that typically didn't accept outsiders, contradictory to the fact that it is a country built by immigrants. Nonetheless, no matter how tough it was, I would not change my experience for anything. I developed a thick skin that has helped me get through so much in my life. I'm not saying what I went through was acceptable or easy, because, as you can imagine, it was tough. However, what I learned was that anything that doesn't break you will make you. I learned to channel all the anger and hurt that I ever faced toward helping others going through what I went through or achieving something great to make my mom happy.

CHAPTER 6

Becoming Americanized

I THINK COMING to America at such a young age made it inevitable that after a while I would become Americanized. I never really declared to myself that I was Americanized until I went back home to Ethiopia. The first time someone told me I was Americanized was when I was complaining about how hot it was. My friend turned and looked at me and said, "What, Mike? You're becoming Americanized, bro! You know it be dumb hot here, you should be used to this." But becoming Americanized was deeper than adjusting to the weather, the language, or anything like that. Becoming Americanized was about embracing the culture as my own or coexisting with the culture and my own. I mainly grew up in Harlem, New York. I moved to the Bronx, New York, when I was in middle school. I continued attend school in Harlem from the second to the twelfth grade while I was still living in the Bronx. Growing up in New York was different from growing up anywhere else in the world, in my opinion. New York City had its own culture, from our demeanor to the way we talked, walked, and even how we dressed.

I attended the University of Bridgeport in Connecticut for college. One of my first jobs in college was working at Ruby Tuesday as a host. I went to the interview wearing slacks and a dress shirt and Prada shoes. One of the servers in the restaurant looked at me and said, "Let me guess. You're from New York." I said, "Yes, how did you know?" She said she could just tell. I was even accused of having a New York accent, and it was mind-boggling, because I didn't really know that people from certain cities had accents. After a year or two in school, I realized there was such a thing. Because my college was one of the most diverse schools in the world, I could distinguish the people who were from Bridgeport and New Haven because they talked differently. The wonderful thing about New York is its beautiful culture and its influence on other cities all over the world. People use New York City culture and make it work for their own. But I was really astonished by the idea of a New York accent. The closer I paid attention to my peers from New York, the more I realized that New Yorkers kind of created a language of their own. We had phrases that were our very own. You knew if anybody said any of the following they were from New York:

"Bro, stop fronting."
"It's brick outside, put your hat on!"
"I'm mad hungry!"
"Why are you being so thirsty?"
"What up, son?"

New Yorkers are famous for coming up with the best slang, and because of emerging social media and music, it usually trends throughout the rest of the world. Some of the best music artists came from New York, and that is a straight fact! ("Fact" is another thing New Yorkers say a lot.) New Yorkers are very proud of their city and what borough they are from. If you see a New Yorker in the midst of an argument, he would instantly mention he is from New York and reasons why you might not want a problem with him. In college, when we have events, they sometimes shout out the names of cities people might be from, and of course you know that New York is the loudest. People not from New York even go crazy. It's funny. New York is truly one of the most diverse places in the world. However, the schools I went to had predominately African American kids, and if I wanted to get along with them I had to become a little Americanized.

Coming to America was really the opportunity of a lifetime. Millions of people around the world seek the opportunity to come to America, so I felt lucky. The day I realized I was becoming Americanized was when I started taking things for granted. I started to compare my life to my friends' lives. I was frustrated about my lack of materialistic items and my lack of freedom. I forgot how fortunate I was to be in America. But since I came to the country at such a young age, I was trying to follow the culture of America instead of my own. My mom would constantly remind me how fortunate I was to be here. She would often tell me horror stories about how difficult it was for her growing up. As much as I listened and tried to understand, I didn't quite understand. I was not listening to understand, but rather I was listening to respond. I couldn't quite connect to what she was talking about, because life in America was different from life in Ethiopia. She constantly told me to never take anything for granted and always take advantage of every opportunity presented to me.

The problem with teenagers is that they don't quite listen to their parents. In high school, I had some of my worst days. My grades didn't reflect my best. I had an all-time low GPA of 2.0; this was unheard of, because my GPA rarely fell below 3.5. However, in high school, I just lost connection with my culture. Even the way I dressed reflected it. I used to sag my pants and involve myself in things that were very uncharacteristic of me. Even getting suspended from school a couple of times, which was definitely not common for me. I worked so hard to always make my family proud, but I didn't feel like anything I did was good enough, and so I just kind of gave up and became careless. I saw my friends being showered with so many things while they were doing far less than I was. On the other hand, I was excelling in various part of my life and didn't get anything. It didn't make sense to me. I started to value materialism, which was something that was not part of my culture. Our parents taught us to value what we had internally, because that was what was most important. The reason was that if we put too much value on materialism, the moment we don't have materialistic items or can no longer afford those things, we begin to feel less insignificant than we truly are. The reason being people let material-istic item determine who they are instead of the content of their character I quickly realized that my actions were hurting my mom and I had to get it together. It was foolish to think that she wasn't proud of me. Even to excel was stupid, because if I wanted to be anything in life and pay my mom back for all the sacrifices she made in her life for me, I would have to work harder and continue to excel to make her proud.

Becoming Americanized wasn't bad at all. I mean, that is what is so special about humanity, we can truly adapt to any environment. In order to be successful in whatever you do, you must be adaptable, and becoming Americanized was my way of adapting. However, did it mean I had to lose my culture because I was adapting to the American culture? Absolutely not! I still had to be true to who I was. Being Ethiopian and of African descent was who I was. There was a point in my life, early on, when I was ashamed to admit to people I was from Africa, because I was scared what they would say to me. The day I became comfortable with who I was and where I came from was the day when I truly found myself. Every time somebody asks where I am from, I say I'm from Ethiopia, which is in Africa. Even though they still say I don't look African, I reply, "You would be amazed how people from Africa look."

It's amazing to me how a couple of years ago I wouldn't even tell people I was African, but now people are accepting people who come from Africa. It gives me hope for humanity; well, at least they are nice to my face about it. Africa has really grown as a continent. Throughout other countries in Africa, people are becoming very innovative with the little resources they have. Even my country, Ethiopia, has grown tremendously. It has one of the fastest growing economies and was even voted as the world's best tourism destination in 2015. When I had the opportunity to go to Ethiopia with my two-way ticket, I was really astonished about everything I saw. The media paints the wrong picture in your head, even if you were born there. There was much construction happening and I saw some beautiful archi-tecture and museums. I saw a diverse population with many tourists and foreigners conducting business in Ethiopia, learning and adapting to the culture. There were many people from China in Ethiopia also. They even spoke Amharic, and that was beautiful to see. As much advancement as I saw, there is still much room for help and improvement in Ethiopia. I saw crippled people who had to crawl, people begging for money, overcrowded hospitals, and much more. I remember I was walking to the hospital my grandmother was in and I saw a group of kids playing with a handmade soccer ball, and it just took me back to a time when I was growing up there and I had to do the exact same thing. I walked over to the nearest grocery store and bought the kids a soccer ball. They were very grateful and even took a picture with me. It was such a humbling experience.

My grandmother entered a lottery for a condo to move from her government home, but she still had not been picked, so we had to use a community bathroom. I was way too Americanized at the time, and my knee had taken a lot of hits from falling so much while playing basketball in my past, so to bend and try to use the bathroom was a struggle. Instead, every morning when I was in Ethiopia, I walked to the hotel by my grandmother's house, which was a five-minute walk, and used the toilet there, where I could comfortably sit down and not worry about falling back or something like that. Come to think of it, the way that Ethiopians and so many people around the world use the bathroom is so much healthier than just sitting on a toilet. The proper way to use the bathroom is to squat. Do you think by squatting to use the bathroom they are misfortunate or smart?

When I came back from Ethiopia to New York, I was really humbled and the experience helped me remember where I came from and get closer to God. My mother always took me and my siblings to church when she wasn't working and running around to support her family. So I was totally disconnected from God when I arrived in Ethiopia. However, when I went to Ethiopia, there was just a feeling of gratitude and gratefulness from everyone I met. Every sentence they spit out had a correlation to God. I visited so many beautiful churches in Ethiopia and there were so many people who had misfortunes such as being handicapped, blind, poor in wealth (I specify "in wealth," because if you have life, you can't be totally poor), or even homeless, but they had such a powerful connection with

God that they knew they would be okay throughout life if they kept their faith and stayed close to their religion.

I vividly remember one night in Ethiopia when I was at my aunt's house and she was very sick. It seemed like that night was going to be her last night on earth. The whole family was gathered, and everyone was fearful and emotional. I remember just sitting there frozen, with tears running down my face, wishing I could do something. I wished I had some kind of superpower where I could touch her and heal her. My family members around me were pleading and begging her to go to the hospital, but she continuously refused. She stated that they would just inject her with something and giver her medicine that never worked. We continued to plead with her, and she continued to say no. Ethiopian homes were often decorated with beautiful religious decorations. My aunt looked up at a poster of God, closed her eyes, and said, "If he wants to heal me, he will heal me, and if he doesn't, then it's my time to serve him outside of this earth." She had such a connection with God that she was okay with whatever the outcome was. When I heard her say everything she said, it was as if I was playing a role in a movie or something. It was so surreal and powerful to watch. She was actually facing death, and instead of rushing to the hospital like any person would, she refused and left it with God. She said the doctor was not more powerful than God. I know people who rush to the hospital for a headache, and here was a woman looking death in the eye and it didn't intimidate her for a second. She urged everyone to leave her alone and let her get some rest. Everyone left her in her room and granted her wish.

But as you can imagine, the difficulty I had sleeping was pretty immense. I just kept replaying everything in my head in amazement. I couldn't wait for the sun to come out so I could run to her house down the street to check on her. I prayed for the best outcome that night, and I managed to get in a couple of hours of sleep. The next day, I rushed to my aunt's house and ran into her room. When I got there, she wasn't there. I got this gut-wrenching feeling and started to get emotional again. I asked my cousin what happened to my aunt and where she was. She said, "Relax, she just went to church this morning." I just smiled and said "wow" in my head. A few minutes later, I heard my aunt's voice, and there was a glow in her face. I looked up to the sky and smiled and thanked God. She made me breakfast that day, and I spent most of the day talking to her about life, religion, and how I was growing up. That day I saw the light and the work of God and I realized how powerful it was to believe.

I am truly grateful for my culture, because it shaped me into the person I am today. I have a great balance with the American culture and my own culture today, and it has helped me excel in all aspects of my life. The Ethiopian culture gives me the discipline I need to maneuver through the obstacles that are thrown at me. It helps me value every opportunity I get and take full advantage of every service I am fortunate to have. The American culture showed me how to hustle, it developed my grind. I studied many people who came from nothing in pursuit of the American dream, and with hard work and dedication they were able to make their dreams come true. When you execute your goals with consistency and dedication, there is nothing you cannot achieve.

Photos from my trip to Ethiopia:

Bought the kids a new ball. #givingback

Passing on the blessing. One of the best moments of my life!

Ethiopian Church

Goat made a great meal. When I took this picture, I knew I was Americanized.

CHAPTER 7

African or African American

Fasten your seat belt, because this might be a controversial chapter. You know, when I was growing up in America, it was tough for me. Everybody made fun of me just for being African. However, as time passed and everyone became accepting of African culture and embraced people from Africa for their culture and customs, everything shifted. When people asked me what race I belonged to, I never said I was black. I would always say I was African. It was not because I was born in Africa, because I have friends born in America with African parents who would not tell you that they were black, they would say they were African. As I got older, I saw these conversations starting to happen more. The conversation about if you were African, did you claim to be black or African American? For example, if you one is filling out a questionnaire and it asks about one ethnicities, do you check African-American or check others and write African? When I was younger this would be a no brainer. I would have to check other and put African. The reason being my peers always reminded me I was not one of them which was African-American I was solely African. When I was growing up the worst thing to be was African, and most of the American kids in school would get a kick out of making fun of me for being African. But now that I am older, when I say I'm African and not black, my African American friends label me ignorant. Now, if we are talking about skin complexion, I am totally black. But when people said I was black or African, it was about what their ethnicity was and what race they represented.

This topic is dear to my heart and I have no bias on either side, because I adopted the African American culture while growing up. I love the culture, the music, the style, the slang, and everything else that comes with it, because there is a history behind everything. I wouldn't say one or another race was better, but there are certain customs I embraced from both my Ethiopian and African American cultures, as I mentioned before. Just like Americans have different stereotypes of Africans, Africans have stereotypes of white Americans and African Americans. When it comes to African stereotypes, back in the early 1990s and 2000s, for white Americans it was nothing but positive. Whether it was on television or they had real encounters face-to-face, it was mostly positive. When white Americans were seen on television by Africans, it was mostly to help or raise money to provide the necessary tools for Africans to thrive. Therefore Africans never had any sort of aniomisty towards white Americans, because we saw them as a resource for help.

On the other hand, the stereotype that Africans had of African Americans was anything but positive. They perceived African Americans to be loud, disrespectful thugs, lazy, violent, etc. The same negative perception was noted among African Americans. They took Africans to be cocky, as if they were better than African Americans; they saw them as kissing up to the "white man"; they always smelled, etc. These misconceptions on both sides came from a lack of education, and certain stereotypes were fueled by the media. Of course, some of this came from experience as well. Growing up, my mother never forbade me from hanging out with people because of their skin color or anything of that sort, but she did always remind me to be careful and judge people only by their character.

The characters I came across among my African American peers were not so positive, though. Growing up, I did not have the best feeling for African Americans, because they were the primary reason I hated my existence when I came to America. They were the ones who insulted me with all kind of names, most notably "African booty scratcher." However, despite the negative encounters I had with African Americans, I have had some positive encounters. In fact, most of my close friends are indeed African American, including my girlfriend. Furthermore, so were my teachers who helped me learn English, some of my peers who stood up for me when I was being bullied, and the kids who helped me adapt to the new culture and accepted my flaws. In the early 1990s and early 2000s, there was a clash between the two races. It got to the point where I plainly lied to people, saying that I was born in America when I was asked about my origin for the first time. And because I didn't fit the stereotypical view of how an African looked, they automatically believed me. One, I was ashamed of who I was, and two, I didn't want to go through the judging and bullying. It wasn't until I got older that I was proud of my culture and admitted my culture and where I was from to people. When people asked me where I was from, I would say I was from Ethiopia. Some people had no idea what continent Ethiopia was in, and so I would just say I was African.

I perceive education to be the key to all understanding between humans. Before I came to America, I had no idea of the kind of adversity and hardships that African Americans faced. When I was in Ethiopia, I didn't know about all the great figures such as Martin Luther King, Malcolm X, Rosa Parks, and all the powerhouse leaders who fought for African Americans in times of oppression, discrimination, and segregation. When I came to learn about the slavery that occurred in America, I was baffled and in disbelief that such inhuman action could take place. All I learned in Ethiopia was how great being in America was. They didn't teach us about the protests and violence that African Americans had to face from white Americans. It wasn't until I started to learn about the mishaps that occurred with African Americans that I started to realize why there was such a divide between white Americans and African Americans. Therefore, I could understand how African Americans would perceive Africans in a negative light when Africans praise the white Americans. However, the thing about the past is that there is nothing we can do to change it. The only thing we can do is learn from it and learn how we can prevent such things from ever happening again.

Often, Africans perceive African Americans as always using "the system" as a reason why they can't advance to the next level. Since Africans don't have too much knowledge about the system that oppressed people in America (or even if they do), they don't see the system as the reason for the lack of advancement or as an excuse for reaching the optimal level in their life. For one, coming to America for any foreigner is an advantage. When foreigners come to America, they want to learn as much as possible and be able to advance to a social class so they can help their families back home. Although the system still has a lot of play when it comes to discriminating against minorities and sexes, we have to be able to position ourselves to be the best possible candidates to advance, whether we are African American or African. If we are the best possible candidate for any position we seek, and we are the best at whatever we do, it's going to be hard for someone to use the system to hold us back. I'm not saying that it won't happen even if you are the best at whatever you do. In the twenty-first century, discrimination and racism are still apparent, but we have to be able to overcome the system and be ready for any opportunity that may come our way.

Not only does "the system" discriminate against us, but we also discriminate among ourselves. Society tries to tell us how we can act, what we can wear, how we can speak, etc. These labels hold us back from uniting to cause change. History has proven that when people unite for a common cause and stick up for what is right, there will certainly be some changes that occur. It might not happen right away, but believe me, it will definitely happen. We have to stop accusing people of stealing our culture and telling them they can't do this or that because they are of a different ethnicity, but tell them to unite when we need people to unite. I go to a very diverse college, and during my time in college, I have been a part of many different movements, such as Black Lives Matter and the protest against President Trump's ban on seven predominantly Muslim countries. I am not one to say that I won't stand for a cause because it doesn't directly affect my ethnicity or religion. I know what is right deep down inside, and as humans, we have to move past the labels that were created in order to separate us and hold us back. I believe in karma wholeheartedly. My mom always taught me while I was growing up that whatever you do in life, whether good or bad, will come back around. Even if it doesn't come in your lifetime, it will be passed down to your kids or other family members.

I know throughout the book I keep saying different races, but truly there is only one race, and that is humanity. The other "races" were created to separate us. We have to look past colors and religion and always focus on what's right. One of the reasons that America is known as the greatest country in the world is the constitutional right it provides for its people to speak openly and protest against the government. In many countries across the world, it might not be common that people can openly protest and bash their government. In certain countries, you might even be apprehended and convicted for protesting against your government. But I grew up in America, where people are constantly protesting the judicial system when it continues to fail people in search of change. So when an issue arises in America or in our communities, we have to strive to be part of the change that happens for better days, not for only us, but for the generation that's going to come after us.

CHAPTER 8

Career Path

REMEMBER THE HILARIOUS memes in chapter 5? Specifically the one about the career path that an African kid could indulge in? One is to be a doctor, two is to be an engineer, three is to be a lawyer, and four is to be a disgrace to the family. While this is funny, there is some truth to it. From the day you are born, you have immense pressure as an African child to live up to all the ridiculously high expectations. You are expected to excel in your academics, go to college and graduate—maintaining a 4.0 GPA for all of your academic career—and make tons of money. Even if your parents don't openly admit it, as kids we know it's important for us to perform well in school to make them proud. When I was in high school before coming to college, I was interested in computer engineering. So from tenth to twelfth grade, I would tell my mom that I was going to be an engineering student, so that one day she would be thrilled about my decision and be proud of me. I was such a mama's boy, I wanted nothing more than to please her and make her happy. I remember she would be on the phone with her friends telling them that I was going to major in engineering when I got to college. I had no idea what computer engineering entailed when I was in high school and the amount of complex classes I would have to endure to obtain a degree. All I knew was that engineering made my mom happy, and how much engineers got paid made me happy.

I worked at my high school cleaning and updating software on the computer. I did a darn good job, and I felt like engineering had nothing on me and it would be a cakewalk. When I started college and dived into my major, it was the hardest wake-up call in my life. It was like jumping off a building and falling flat on the ground. I might be exaggerating, but that's how I felt. As DJ Khaled would say, "I played myself"! The classes I had to endure the first two semesters were tough. I hated every class. Nothing they talked about caught my attention, nor was I able to comprehend anything they were talking about. God forbid that I blink my eyes during a lecture in class, I would be totally lost. I missed out on so many activities with my friends, because I had to lock myself up in my room or the library trying to catch up on the work. I didn't realize that with a major like engineering, you have to have some sort of knowledge about it before college. Most of the kids in my class had been coding and were geniuses in mathematics, so the major was not too bad for them. My GPA suffered because I had trouble comprehending most of the material in class. I was playing catch-up through most of the class. Engineering for me was basically someone trying to teach me how to walk before I learned how to crawl. I didn't really want to change my major, because I had told my family since high school that I would be an engineer and would be successful. Also, the biggest factor for me sticking to my major was not wanting to disappoint my mother.

I had to change my major, because if I didn't my GPA would fall way below the requirement to keep some of my scholarship in school. Eventually I mustered the courage and I called my mother to tell her that I was going to change my major. She asked if I was switching to be a doctor. I had no interest in the healthcare industry. My mother was a registered nurse, so she wanted me to be a doctor. I told her I was switching my major to business management. She took it better than I expected. I was relieved that she wasn't so mad at my decision. I had held off seeing my advisor to switch my major until I consulted with my mother. As soon as I got the go-ahead from my mom, I was thrilled to switch my major. My advisor asked, "Are you sure, Mike?" I said I had never been so sure in my life! I knew since I was young that I was destined for greatness. It didn't bother me much to have to switch my major, nor did it feel like I would not be successful now that I switched my major. Being successful was my only choice, not only to make my family proud, but to help the family I had in Ethiopia. I knew they were waiting for me to graduate and get a job so that I would be able to support them financially. I'm not sure they would have taken it well if they had realized the pay difference between a business manager and an engineer.

When I switched my major to business, everything clicked. My GPA started to skyrocket from before and I was truly learning and embracing everything I was getting inside the classroom. When I transitioned into the business school, the entrepreneur in me was born. I started my clothing line, called No Sleep. I was excited, I felt like I was going to be the next Ralph Lauren or something. No Sleep was more than a clothing line to me, it was a representation that if you give up sleep and channel your energy into working on your dreams and goals, you can ultimately be successful one day. It was inspired by the countless videos by motivational speaker Eric Thomas that I had listened to. Every time I finished listening to him, I would have a new refreshing energy. It was like, "Whoa! No sleep!" At the time I started my brand, I literally was not getting any sleep. It took a lot of coffee and Red Bull to get me through the day. I was a resident advisor, I was heavily involved on campus, and I was working to pay for school.

When I presented the idea for my company to my mother, she was not the most supportive person. It wasn't that she didn't believe in me and the brand, she just didn't support entrepreneurship. Looking back at it now, I can't really blame her. She was never really exposed to that sort of thing when she was growing up. All she knew was to work hard and get a good job working for someone. She was not very optimistic about all the risk factors that had to do with entrepreneurship. She felt like I was basically throwing my money away and I should just be saving instead. It was tough for me to have to listen to this, but it didn't deter me from going after my passion. So with the help of a friend, I designed T-shirts and got them manufactured. I set up the website and I created hype on social media. When I was promoting the shirts, everybody around me was excited and said, "I was excited to buy a shirt, but when it was time to buy, they were not around." The few people who were willing to get a shirt were asking for discounts. The same friends who spent two hundred dollars plus on a pair of sneakers. Of course, I had people around me and strangers who were willing to support me no matter the cost, because they believed in my brand and vision.

However, instead of focusing my time on the people who supported me, I focused on the people who didn't support me. I focused my time on the people who said they would support me and didn't support me. I later learned that was a terrible thing. I have to channel my time and allocate my energy to people who only want to see me win. I was scrolling on social media once and saw a post that explained exactly everything I felt. The post said, "Do you know why strangers support you more than people you know? Because some people you know are having a hard time accepting that you both came from the same place and they are still in the same place." When I read this, I was in awe, because I couldn't have said it any better. I always had haters growing up, and this it was nothing new, but it seemed that when I got to college, they came in the disguise of friends. The funny thing was, I had friends who were thrilled to see how far I had come, see a kid who knew no English attain the level I had gotten to. Nevertheless, it was a tough life lesson. I was selling the shirts for about fifteen dollars and it cost me about nine dollars to make them. I just wanted to spread the message to people. It helped me develop an unbelievable work ethic, and I was not willing to accept failure, so I spent every chance I got working. Even when I was sleeping I was working, I was dreaming about T-shirt designs and ways to grow my brand.

Over the span of a few months, I was writing my book, and I would get hit with so many story ideas and wake up and write them in my notes. I mean, that's just how badly I wanted to win. A lot of times, even if you deserve to win, it doesn't mean anything unless you put in the work, and even then, you still might not win. A lot of people tell me I'm destined to win and be successful. If I had a dollar every time someone told me not to forget them when I make it big, I would have accumulated a lot toward my savings. The way I got that recognition was through hard work and dedication. No matter how destined you are, and even if your name is Destiny, you will never manifest your success if you don't work toward whatever craft and career you want to get into.

African Booty Scratcher

During my junior year of college in 2016, I started a new business idea. During one of my marketing classes, the professor asked us to come up with a new business idea. It was like a gift from God. I came up with an idea for a "Netflix for textbooks." I presented the idea to my class, and the whole class loved the idea. My school had an entrepreneur center to help students bring their projects to life. So I felt like I had a gold mine, and I immediately signed up for the program and started the journey. I told my parents about this idea and they liked it. But I didn't get the reaction that I was looking for from my mom again. I couldn't blame her, because my T-shirt business didn't do so well, and she was not so optimistic about my next entrepreneurial journey.

Anyway, just like the T-shirt, I failed a lot with my new business, Superior eBook, a Netflix for textbooks model. I realized that there was a reason such a model didn't exist. Traditional book companies were making so much money dishing out new editions of books and making students buy them for hundreds of dollars. In business, there is something called a pivot. A pivot just means taking a new direction when your initial business plan is not working out, so you resort to plan B. I used numerous plan Bs and I'm still working on my business. It's easy to give up when you're not succeeding and your plan B seem worse than your plan A. But that is when you have to find your "why"! Why do you do what you do? Why do you wake up every day? I once heard a quote that really stuck with me: "The two most important days in your life are the day you are born and the day you find out why you were born. Once you find your *why*, you will then become unstoppable." Sometime I get mad at myself and I feel, why can I not have regular dreams like my friends? Why can I not dream of average things like my friends and get fewer disappointments and tears on my pillow? But then I think about my "why" and I keep going. I think about all the kids who bullied me for not being materialistic and having name-brand items. It motivates me to work harder to get things I couldn't have when I was younger and provide my family with the life they deserve. What's my "why"? You're going to find out soon. You should know half of it already.

Nonetheless, finding your career path is just about manifesting your future. I always talk about things as if I've already obtained them. I remember entering a business plan competition for my business. I already saw myself winning the competition. I worried less about the competition and more about how I was going to distribute the money I would win in my business. I didn't even make it to the finale both times I manifested this. However, that didn't deter me from continuing to manifest things as existing, because you have to be the biggest supporter of your own brand. When things don't work out in your favor, it should always push you to work a lot harder. I attribute my success in life to the many failures and knockdowns I've experienced.

One of my goals for my senior year of college was to obtain a 4.0 grade point average. I was sure I was going to obtain it, and yet again I failed. I got a 3.98 grade point average because of one A-minus I got in one of my classes. But what would have happened if I did get my 4.0 GPA? I might have slacked off the following semester. The hurt and failure I experience just motivates me to keep going.

I know that it's easier said than done. Trust me, I know. I would listen to motivational speakers and they would talk about how much they loved not succeeding because it pushed them to go harder. It would stick with me for a moment, and then I would look at them and think, They are already millionaires. It's much tougher for a struggling kid who can't afford to take the same amount of Lossesthat a millionaire can withstand. And I'm not taking anything from successful wealthy people, because they all had to go through hell and work immeasurable hours to obtain the success that they have. But it's hard for people to understand the success you haven't yet obtained, because they would give up everything they have to live the lifestyle the millionaire has. Failures and struggles are going to be what makes your success much sweeter. Also, it's important to look at someone's success and use it as a standard, but everyone has their own pathway to success. If you focus on what other people have and why you haven't achieved the success they have achieved, you're paying way too much attention to them. It's great to study people so you understand the routine they undertook to get to the level of success they have, but you have to write your own book and live the lifestyle you deserve.

CHAPTER 9

❧

Mom

So what's my "why"? My mother is my "why." On August 1, 2016, I lost my mother to breast cancer. It was one of the most horrific days of my life. From that day forward, my life changed forever. When my mother passed away, so did a piece of me. I cried for days upon days wondering how and why such a tragedy could occur. I questioned everything, especially my faith. I just could not comprehend how she was taken from my life when I was on my way to repay her for all the sacrifices she had ever made for me. I was entering my senior year of college when she passed away, and I couldn't wait for graduation. I had high hopes that I would be the commencement speaker for my class, so that I could get on the stage and tell my class and the world what a superwoman my mother was. Growing up, I watched her struggle to take care of her family while working and going to school full time to be a nurse. I remember how little sleep she would get, and she would come home so I could tell her about all the problems I was having in school. I look back at it now and think, how could I have been such a fool and stress her with my minimal problems when she had way bigger fish to fry?

When she passed away, I knew she was going to a better place where she didn't have to suffer anymore. But still I didn't get a chance to buy her the house that she wanted, and she didn't get a chance to see all of her hard work pay off with me. I know the cliché that she is looking down on me with pride, but I would give anything to look her in the eye, kiss her and hug her, and tell her how eternally grateful I am to her. I remember a week before she passed away, she was in pain and I was holding on to her, crying. She urged me to be strong and promised me everything will be fine.

She said, "I know you are going to be successful and I have other people counting on you to be successful whether I am here or not." She urged me to never give up and to tackle any adversity that comes my way. When she told me that, I just cried even more. I couldn't understand life without my mom. Even when I went away to college, I never went more than two or three days without speaking to her. When she passed away, everything we had talked about flashed across my mind.

When my mother passed away, it would have been easy for me to just give up everything I had going for me and say I could no longer keep going because I was a child without a mother. After a couple of days, I knew I had to get back on my feet and work toward being as successful as possible. The summer my mom passed away, I got one of the first outside scholarships I ever received. I smiled, because I knew she had something to do with it, and after a while I truly did feel like my mother was looking down on me, watching every step I take. Sometimes I would go to sleep and wake up thinking it was a dream, that she didn't really pass away. But it was indeed the reality. Not only do I have her to keep going for, I have two younger siblings, my little man who is five, his name is Semere, and my little sister, Fetun, who is eight. My mother gave up everything for me and my family. The reason I even started to write this book was because of her. I want the world to know the kind of woman she was and the kind of son she helped create.

I love you, mom. I will never stop trying to make you proud.

CHAPTER 10

Reflection

WOULD I HAVE changed the circumstances and the way I grew up? Would I have wanted a life without bullying when I was younger? Would I have wanted to come from wealthier parents? Would I have wanted non-African parents? Absolutely not. I would never have formed into the Michael Asmerom I am now. The funny thing about life is that everything you experience and all the hard work you put in always has results. It might take some time and you might feel like giving up, but I promise you it will do a 180-degree turn and make all the blood, sweat, and tears worth it. Also, the same is true if you're not putting in the work and you're constantly posting about the life you want, with no execution. If you're not executing your goals on a daily basis, you will never be able to live the lifestyle you dream about. You will spend more time fantasizing about people and the life you want to live instead of actually working toward your goals and dreams. The problem with my generation and those before me is that we have fallen victim to instant gratification: we want results right away.

It's not going to happen, and when it does happen it's very rare. We are growing up in era when things are becoming a lot less time-consuming with the advancement of technology. With a click of a button we can order food, get transportation, make payments, watch movies, etc. However, one thing that's never going to change is the amount of time you will need to put in in order to be successful. There is no such thing as an overnight success. Every overnight success took years in the making. They just did something the night before that put them over the edge. All of the most successful people you know in your life or through the media put hours upon hours into their craft, and when there was a platform to showcase their talent, they showed up. However, had they not spent countless hours perfecting their craft and giving up friends and activities that would slow them down, you might not ever know them. What would have happened if Michael Jordan gave up once he got cut from his high school basketball team? Can you imagine that? Probably one of the greatest things that happened to him was getting cut from that team. He went back to the lab and worked countless hours to become the G.O.A.T. (greatest of all time). Sometimes, whether we know it or not, failing and getting hurt can be a blessing in disguise. What would have happened if I had the perfect childhood and never got bullied? I would have been just a regular person with no story to tell to inspire or change someone's life.

Life gives everyone a process. My mentor tells me all the time that there's no elevator to success, you've got take the steps. Every step you take in life has a lesson and a reasoning that's going to help you with the next step. Everything I ever learned and failed at in life continues to help me get stronger and overcome the next adversity. I wish I understood that notion when I was growing up. Maybe I would have smiled every time I cried and felt pain, because I would have known that was the fuel I needed to take me to the next level.

I remember when I was younger how much I wished I had American parents. They would tell me they always wished they had a child like me. I remember thinking, I'm up for getting adopted. It was never that my mom took me for granted or didn't appreciate that she had a son like me. It was more that she never wanted to let me feel comfortable with anything. She didn't spend a lot of time celebrating any success I achieved; it was always on to the next one. Looking back at it now, I am beyond grateful for every bully I ever had in my life, every no I heard in my life, and I'm even grateful for all the whopping I ever got growing up. They all helped shape me into the person I am today. When I was growing up, I used to question everything. I used to feel, why do I have to live in certain circumstances and why I don't have the freedom that my American friends have? Now, as I reflect on everything that has ever occurred in my life, I see there was a reason behind it all, maybe even being called an African booty scratcher.

Acknowledgments

FIRST AND FOREMOST, thank you to God for pushing me through the rigorous process of completing a book. Thank you to my mother for all the sacrifice and work she put into me to make me the man I am today. I want to thank my stepdad, Shimles Assefa, for always staying by my side and encouraging me. I am eternally grateful for the care that he gave my mom when she was battling cancer. Thank you to my older sister for always being a friend and super supportive of everything I do in life. Thank you to all my friends and family members who stood by my side in times of hardship and continue to push me to greatness.

46707221R00050

Made in the USA
Middletown, DE
07 August 2017